Gumdrop Bks. 9/03/03 22.95

Critical Thinking About
Environmental Issues

Endangered
Species

Critical Thinking About
Environmental Issues

Endangered
Species

Other books in the Critical Thinking About
Environmental Issues series include:

Global Warming
Pesticides

Critical Thinking About
Environmental Issues

Endangered Species

by Randy T. Simmons

Jane S. Shaw, *Series Editor*
Senior Associate
PERC, The Center for Free
Market Environmentalism

GREENHAVEN
PRESS ®

THOMSON
™
GALE

San Diego • Detroit • New York • San Francisco • Cleveland
New Haven, Conn. • Waterville, Maine • London • Munich

For more information, contact
Greenhaven Press
27500 Drake Rd.
Farmington Hills, MI 48331-3535
Or you can visit our Internet site at http://www.gale.com

LIBRARY OF CONGRESS CATALOGING-IN-PUBLICATION DATA

Simmons, Randy T.
  Endangered species / by Randy T. Simmons.
    p. cm. — (Critical thinking about environmental issues)
Summary: Investigates how serious the threat is to certain species called endangered, the effectiveness of the Endangered Species Act, global responsibility to protect plants and animals, and future concerns.
Includes bibliographical references and index.
  ISBN 0-7377-1266-X (hardback : alk. paper)
  1. Endangered species—Juvenile literature. [1. Endangered species.] I. Title. II. Critical thinking about environmental issues series.
  QH75.S54 2002
  333.95'22—dc21

                                      2002001265

Contents

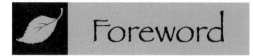

Foreword

If a nation expects to be ignorant and free . . . it expects
what never was and never will be.

—Thomas Jefferson

Thomas Jefferson understood that a free nation depends on
an educated citizenry. Citizens must have the level of
knowledge necessary to make informed decisions on complex public policy issues. In the United States, schools have a major
responsibility for developing that knowledge.

In the twenty-first century, American citizens will struggle with
environmental questions of the first order. These include complicat-
ed and contentious topics such as global warming, pesticide use, and
species extinction. The goal of this series, Critical Thinking About
Environmental Issues, is to help young people recognize the com-
plexity of these topics and help them view the issues analytically and
objectively.

All too often, environmental problems are treated as moral issues.
For example, using pesticides is often considered bad because
residues may be found on food and because the application of pesticides may harm birds. In contrast, relying on organic food (pro-
duced without insecticides or herbicides) is considered good. Yet this
simplistic approach fails to recognize the role of pesticides in pro-
ducing food for the world and ignores the scientific studies that suggest that pesticides cause little harm to humans. Such superficial
treatment of multifaceted issues does not serve citizens well and provides a poor basis for education.

This series, Critical Thinking About Environmental Issues, expos-
es students to the complexities of each issue it addresses. While the
books touch on many aspects of each environmental problem, their
goal is primarily to point out the differences in scientific opinion
surrounding the topics. These books present the facts that underlie
different scientific interpretations. They also address differing values
that may affect the interpretation of the facts and economic questions that may affect policy choices.

The goal of the series is to open up inquiry on issues that are often
viewed too narrowly. Each book, written in language that is under-

standable to young readers, provides enough information about the scientific theories and methods for the reader to weigh the merits of the leading arguments. Ultimately, students, like adult citizens, will make their own decisions.

With environmental issues, especially those where new science is always emerging, the possibility exists that there is not enough information to settle the issue. If this is the case, the books may spur readers to pursue the topics further. If readers come away from this series critically examining their own opinions as well as others' and eager to seek more information, the goal of these books will have been achieved.

by Jane S. Shaw
Series Editor

INTRODUCTION

A re humans eradicating the earth's plant and animal life and creating a "planet of weeds,"[1] as one writer phrases it? If so, will the future be bereft of wild lions, tigers, elephants, and monkeys—except for those captive in zoos?

The answer is not a simple one. Clearly, human activities, the growth of population, and the development of cities and towns pose a threat to animals and plants. But the actual condition of the world's species is difficult to know for certain. Although some species are in danger and some extinct, others, from the bald eagle to the Bengal tiger, are rebounding or holding steady.

Thanks to preservation efforts by governments and conservation organizations, there is hope for the beautiful Bengal tiger.

Protecting endangered species is both a scientific and a political challenge. Scientists differ on how many species are heading for extinction, and therefore whether the world faces a crisis of extinction. Only research will ultimately answer the question.

At the same time, actions taken to preserve plants and animals can affect the lives of many people, especially in rural areas, where endangered species are most likely to be found. Sometimes it appears that a conflict exists between people and animals.

The United States has a law, the Endangered Species Act, that is designed to protect species. Yet, there is much debate over whether it is effective. Its implementation can affect those unlucky people who may have endangered species on their property. Some of the conflicts over the Endangered Species Act raise the question of whether there are other ways besides passing laws to help protect species.

As with other environmental problems, such as global warming, scientists have much to learn. Important scientific questions are never easy to understand and resolve, but they are interesting and exciting. The purpose of this book is to investigate many sides of the endangered species controversies so that readers can come to their own conclusions.

CHAPTER 1

How Endangered Are the World's Species?

In the early part of the nineteenth century, passenger pigeons were so plentiful in the United States that no one thought they could ever disappear. Flocks of these birds were so large that they darkened the sky as they flew over. In 1810, Alexander Wilson, a naturalist, claimed that he saw a flock in Kentucky with more than 2 billion birds. The flock, he said, was a mile wide and 240 miles long.

By the 1890s, however, it was hard to find a passenger pigeon, and by 1914 they had all disappeared. Human settlement had replaced much of their habitat, and the pigeons had been hunted for food. Millions of the birds had been shipped to cities, where they were eaten much the same way as Americans eat chickens today.

The passenger pigeon has come to symbolize extinction. Many people think that such disappearances may be happening today at a rapid pace, one that will accelerate in the future. Says journalist David Hosansky, "The world is facing the largest wave of plant and animal extinctions since the demise of the dinosaurs 65 million years ago."[2] Yet others are skeptical. Bjørn Lomborg, a Danish statistician, says, "Although these assertions of massive extinctions of species have been repeated everywhere you look, they simply do not equate with the facts."[3]

Although the severity of extinction is debatable, the knowledge that humans contribute to it is not. Human actions cause extinctions in several ways. The action that causes the most extinctions seems to be introducing nonnative species and diseases. Although plants and animals can move into new environments by themselves, the transfer of nonnative species comes primarily through international travel, as species move across the oceans in ships or by air.

For example, the European zebra mussel was apparently introduced in the ballast water of ships that sailed into the Great Lakes from Europe through the St. Lawrence River. Once there, it was carried by barges throughout rivers in the central United States. This

The now-extinct passenger pigeon once numbered in the billions in the eastern United States. Hunting and habitat loss quickly drove it to extinction.

mussel and another nonnative mollusk, the Asiatic clam, appear to have caused the extinction of various species of freshwater mussels in rivers that feed into the Gulf of Mexico and the Atlantic Ocean.

Kudzu, now famous as a comic strip, is a fast-growing vine brought from Japan for the American centennial celebration in Philadelphia in 1876. It became popular among gardeners in the 1920s, and the Soil Conservation Service planted it to stop erosion. But it grows so fast—under some conditions, a foot a day—that it can kill trees by keeping out sunlight.

Kudzu, zebra mussels, melaleuca (a tree from Australia), gypsy moths, Africanized bees, and starlings are among the forty-five hundred nonnative species invading habitat in the United States, according to a study by the Congressional Research Service. Author David Quammen says that nonnatives "take hold in strange places, succeed

Fast-growing kudzu vines cover these trees in the American countryside. Like many other species introduced into North America from abroad, the kudzu vine threatens native species.

especially in disturbed ecosystems, and resist eradication once they're established."[4] Some years ago, the World Resources Institute conducted an analysis of the world's known extinctions since 1600. It concluded that 39 percent were caused by the introduction of non-native species.

Almost as lethal are the changes humans make to the land and its vegetation. About 36 percent of the known extinctions since 1600 came through such actions, which include cutting down forests, building cities, and draining wetlands. Farmers in a tropical area may convert a section of rain forest to cropland; a growing city may replace cropland with commercial and residential buildings. These changes in the habitat can make it difficult or impossible for some animals and plants to survive there.

The decline in red-cockaded woodpeckers illustrates the result. When colonists arrived in the seventeenth century, pine forests covered as much as 92 million acres in what is now the southeastern United States, stretching from Virginia to Arkansas. Now they cover about 1.8 million acres and are broken into small parcels. The red-cockaded woodpecker not only inhabits this forest but also builds its nests primarily in holes in large old pine trees. In addition, the woodpecker prefers trees that have a clear understory or open area around them. (This is the kind of habitat that occurs when fires occasionally burn through an area but leave big old trees standing.) Trees that meet all these conditions—pine forests, old trees, and clear understory—are increasingly rare, and that fact has hurt the red-cockaded woodpecker.

Third, hunting and fishing contribute to extinction. According to the World Resources Institute survey, hunting has eliminated 23 percent of the known extinct species since 1600.

Sometimes people deliberately hunt down a species because it is seen as a pest. Wolves were wiped out in Yellowstone National Park early in the twentieth century, for example. They were considered a hazard to more desirable game animals such as deer, elk, and antelope, and nearby ranchers feared them because they ate sheep and calves. Together, rangers and ranchers eradicated the wolf by 1930. (The wolves did not become extinct, but they were no longer found in the park and the surrounding region.) The Carolina parakeet, too, was hunted to extinction by 1920 because it was seen as a pest. The

American bison graze in a national park. Once numbering in the millions, bison were overhunted until only a few hundred remained.

American bison was heavily hunted, although it never became extinct. Its numbers fell from millions in the early nineteenth century to a few hundred animals at the end of the century. The deepwater and black-fin cisco, two fish that were native to Lakes Michigan and Huron, were overfished to the point of extinction.

Overhunting goes back thousands of years. When humans started arriving at islands in the Pacific about three thousand years ago, they found birds that had been almost entirely free of predators. Many were large creatures that could not fly. They were easy to catch when the first inhabitants arrived. According to modern research, more than two thousand island bird species became extinct.

Later, Europeans also discovered bird species when they arrived at unfamiliar islands, especially remote ones. In 1507, for example, they found the dodo on Mauritius, an island in the Indian Ocean. Dodos weighed up to thirty pounds, had little fear of humans, and were very tasty. They were all extinct by 1681. One-third of the fifty native species of Hawaiian land birds that Europeans found there disappeared in the two centuries after European settlement.

Are Humans Causing a Mass Extinction?

The ability of humans to destroy species is clear. Now many scientists worry that a mass extinction of species is occurring. The editor of *Conservation Biology Digest* claims that we could be in the midst of "an extinction episode of historic proportions."[5] Yet others contend that extinction rates are low enough to not be disastrous. Bjørn Lomborg calls the problem of extinction "not a catastrophe but a problem—one of many that mankind still needs to solve."[6] He thinks that relatively minor adjustments to human choices and lifestyles can avert future problems.

Scientists are not alarmed when a few animals die, or small groups of animals move from one site to another, or a field of grassland is replaced by a parking lot. What concerns them is the reduction of formerly large populations to tiny, fragmentary groups that may not be able to survive over time. Biologists are concerned about three categories: species, subspecies, and distinct populations. The most important loss is of a species. This term refers to animals and plants

A drawing of a dodo bird is all that remains of this species driven to extinction before the invention of photography. Its tasty flesh was its downfall.

This northern spotted owl belongs to a subspecies of spotted owl threatened by logging operations in the Pacific Northwest.

that are basically alike; it is the fundamental biological classification that distinguishes one type of plant or animal from another.

About 1.4 million species have been recorded. Scientists think there are many more but they do not know how many, partly because there are different ways of counting species. The elephants in Africa are recognized as different species from those in India. But are the elephants that live in Africa's forests a different species than the ones that live on Africa's savannahs, the open areas with grass and some trees? Or are they both members of the same species? Experts disagree.

Another reason for not knowing how many species there are is that it may be impossible to find and record every species in every ecological niche in the world. For example, there may be as many as 1.6 million species of fungi alone. There may be 10 million species of plants and animals on the ocean floor! The best scientists can do is make educated guesses for the total number of species. These range from 3 million to 100 million.

Scientists are worried about more than species. Subspecies are groups within species that can be distinguished from one another. Distinct populations are groups of varying sizes that are geographically separate from other members of their species or subspecies.

In 1990, the northern spotted owl made news across the United States because the federal government listed it as a threatened species (that is, nearly endangered). To protect it, a federal court, and then the Clinton administration, halted logging on millions of acres of national forests, an act that caused sawmills to close and many workers to lose their jobs. Most of the public called the bird the "spotted owl" and assumed that a species was approaching extinction. Few realized that the decision affected just one of three subspecies of the spotted owl. The other two subspecies are the California and the Mexican spotted owl. They were not in trouble, at least not to the same extent as the northern spotted owl.

Another example of a sub-species is the Mount Graham red squirrel, one of about twenty-five subspecies of red squirrel. The Mount Graham red squirrel became famous in 1988 when researchers proposed building seven astronomical telescopes on Mount Graham, a peak in the Pinaleno Mountains of southeastern Arizona. Opponents

About 1.4 million species have been recorded, but scientists think there are many more.

of the telescopes argued that the Mount Graham squirrels are a distinct population that should be protected. Although a great deal of controversy followed, only three of the proposed seven telescopes have been built.

A Mass Extinction?

For every species alive today, perhaps a thousand lived previously and are extinct. We only know about extinct species from their fossils, their impressions embedded in rock. These fossils show that extinction is a natural part of the evolutionary process and has been going on for as long as there has been life on the earth.

Scientists generally agree that there have been five great extinctions during the earth's history. The first occurred about 440 million

This scene from El Yunque rain forest in eastern Puerto Rico exemplifies the stunning lushness of the rain forest. Rain forest destruction is a serious worldwide environmental issue.

years ago, and the most recent was about 65 million years ago, possibly caused by an asteroid. It took between 10 million and 100 million years after each mass extinction for biodiversity to recover to its previous level.

The chief reason behind the fear that another mass extinction is occurring is the fact that tropical rain forests, considered the richest habitats in the world, are being cut down. Although rain forests can be found throughout the globe where there is high annual rainfall (including Alaska), the rain forests that are endangered are the broad jungles in warm, damp regions of Central and South America, Africa, and southern Asia.

In these areas, forests are being converted to farmland or being cut for timber. The United Nations Food and Agriculture Organization estimates that the tropical rain forest has been cut down or converted at a rate of about 0.45 percent per year. This is lower than the estimates in the 1980s, which were about 0.8 percent of the total acreage every year. It may not sound like very much, but if the losses continue, they accumulate rapidly, even at half a percentage point per year.

Edward O. Wilson is pretty specific about what he thinks is happening in the rain forests. He says that "the number doomed each year is 27,000. Each day it is 74, and each hour 3." His precision may be a rhetorical flourish to emphasize his point, but he is serious. When he adds the rain-forest extinctions to others that he believes are occurring in the rest of the world, he concludes that worldwide extinctions may be at more than 100 per day worldwide. Wilson calls this "the worst wave of extinction since the dinosaurs died."[7]

Others echo his assertion and repeat similar numbers. Michael J. Novacek, the provost of science at the American Museum of Natural History, has said that "figures approaching 30 percent extermination of all species by the mid-21st century are not unrealistic."[8]

But are these claims of mass extinction correct? Although they are widely repeated, there is plenty of debate over whether these rates are realistic. Most scientists agree that extinction rates are greater than they would be in the absence of human actions, but they do not necessarily envision numbers along the lines of Wilson's predictions.

Some years ago, economist Julian L. Simon and political scientist Aaron Wildavsky tried to find the source of the estimates of fifty thousand species lost per year. They couldn't find scientific support for the claims. They traced the origin of these large numbers to a book by Norman Myers, *The Sinking Ark*, written in 1979, in which Myers said that forty thousand species a year may be going extinct. They concluded that he didn't have firm grounding for the estimate and decided it was "pure guesswork."[9] Simon and Wildavsky did not claim that the species are not disappearing, they simply pointed out that the estimates seemed to be based on assumptions, not on facts.

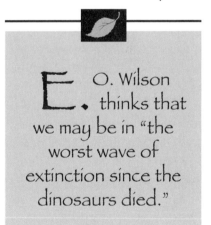

E. O. Wilson thinks that we may be in "the worst wave of extinction since the dinosaurs died."

Others share this skepticism. Reviewing the proliferation of claims made during the 1980s—statements such as the claim that 20 percent of the earth's species would be gone by the year 2000 or that 1 million species would disappear by then—authors Charles C. Mann and

Mark Plummer observed that "many of them seem to have been plucked from thin air."[10]

Predicting Extinctions

Biologists do have a formal way of estimating how many species may be disappearing, but it is based on narrow studies that may not be applicable to worldwide extinction of species. Edward O. Wilson helped develop what is called the "species-area relationship." This is an estimate or rule of thumb about how many species will decline when an area of habitat is reduced. It is expressed in percentage terms, but it is not a rigid number. If 90 percent of a forest is cut down and converted to farmland, for example, this species-area relationship predicts that between 10 and 50 percent of the species will disappear from the land. In other words, not all the species will disappear, but a sizable portion will. The precise proportion depends on the kind of habitat. Scientists study different kinds of habitat (different terrain and vegetation) to determine more precisely what those percentages are.

The species-area relationship was developed by scientists who actually broke up tiny islands of mangrove trees off the southern coast of Florida to find out what would happen to the species on them. In one experiment, the scientists meticulously counted all insect species they could find and then contracted with a pest control company to fumigate the islands. They then monitored how long it took for the insects to recover (it took about a year). In a second experiment, insect species were counted, and then one-third to one-half of each island was cut up with chain saws and hauled away in barges. For the next two years, the scientists counted the insect species. They found out that some never returned, concluding that the number of species was related to the size of the island, "independent of habitat diversity."[11]

Ever since, biologists have argued that there is a predictable reduction in species when habitat area is reduced, and some, like Edward O. Wilson, have applied the number very broadly, as when he concludes that twenty-seven thousand rain-forest species are doomed each year. Such claims depend on many assumptions, such as that we know how many species exist in the rain forest in the first place!

Another assumption is that the habitat has changed so drastically that it is equivalent to the disappearance of part of an island, as in one of the original experiments. Whether forests that become farmland or prairies that become suburbs are the equivalent of destroyed islands isn't at all certain.

So, although the species-area relationship is widely used to measure species loss, many biologists criticize it. One of these is Daniel Simberloff, one of the original researchers cutting up parts of islands to test the theory. He says that "area is a very crude predictor" and "people should be extremely cautious about these predictions, which they sometimes aren't."[12]

The Atlantic coastal forest of Brazil illustrates the difficulties of relying on the species-area relationship to make broad generalizations. Ninety percent of that forest has been cleared in the past five hundred years. If the species-area relationship is applied to this rain forest, up to half of the species there at the time of Columbus should now be extinct. Yet zoologists studying those forests have found no evidence that *any* species went extinct.

The actual facts are not always so rosy. A.H. Gentry studied a small forested mountain ridge in Ecuador that had been cleared for farming. He reported that ninety species of animals and plants had disappeared from the ridge. Fortunately, when he went back for two short

Australia's Daintree rain forest, pictured here, is not only beautiful, it is also home to many species found nowhere else in the world.

An artist's rendering of the ivory-billed woodpecker, one of five bird species that have gone extinct in the eastern United States since 1620.

visits six years later, he found that seventeen of the species he had assumed to be lost were back.

According to the International Union for the Conservation of Nature (IUCN), which published an extensive study of endangered species in 1992, the *known* number of species extinctions in all tropical forests is just one per year. This is far less than what is predicted by the species-area relationship. Thus, efforts to identify actual extinctions, rather than calculate theoretical extinctions, often result in much smaller numbers.

Among its other activities, the IUCN records species that are extinct, endangered, and threatened. It publishes the IUCN Red List, which is a documentation of all the known animal and plant extinctions since 1600. It has documented 644 animal extinctions since 1600. Animals on the list include New Zealand's moas, large flightless birds that stood six to nine feet tall and weighed more than four hundred pounds; the Great Lakes' blackfin and deepwater cisco, 15 million tons of which were harvested from one lake in 1885; and the Bourbon crested starling from the Island of Reunion off the coast of Africa. There have been 396 plant extinctions.

Looking at precise numbers this way gives a different picture of species extinction. The IUCN can identify only about one thousand extinctions over the past four hundred years. Although some extinctions have undoubtedly been missed, the numbers suggest that so far at least human actions have not had a catastrophic impact on plant and animal diversity.

Other evidence, too, supports the idea that the extinctions have not been drastic, suggesting that future extinctions may not be as severe as some expect. East of the Mississippi River, for example, there were as many as 600 million acres of forest when the Pilgrims arrived in the United States in 1620. At that time, the forest contained about 160 species of birds, but by 1950, the forest was half that size. It has increased in the past fifty years, but many of the remaining parts are in fragmented patches. What happened to the birds?

Today, 5 of the estimated 160 species are extinct. Two of them—the ivory-billed woodpecker and Bachman's warbler —most likely disappeared due to deforestation. The passenger pigeon was hunted to extinction (although it also lost habitat), and the Carolina parakeet was extensively hunted because farmers viewed it as a pest—it gathered in great flocks that destroyed crops. The combination of hunting and deforestation drove the parakeet to extinction. The heath hen succumbed to hunting pressure, but

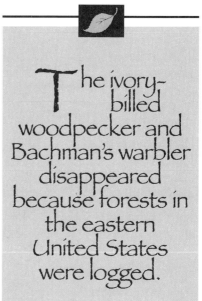

The ivory-billed woodpecker and Bachman's warbler disappeared because forests in the eastern United States were logged.

it also lost habitat. The hen preferred meadows scattered through forests, the kind of habitat that comes from periodic fires. As settlers suppressed more and more fires, the forests grew thicker and many open areas disappeared.

Dozens of other bird species exist in the eastern United States. Some, like the chestnut-sided warbler, are found in far greater numbers than when John James Audubon first recorded seeing one. Others, like the piping plover, are threatened with extinction.

The Nature Conservancy and Environmental Defense reported in 1994 that their survey of plants and animals in the Pacific Northwest revealed no actual extinctions of plants or animals since 1945. Some populations are in decline, and some Pacific salmon runs are dangerously low. However, as journalist Gregg Easterbrook reports, this region "has not only been subjected to extensive logging but also numbers among the most intensely studied in the world and is therefore a place where extinctions are likely to be detected."[13] The fact that there are no known recent extinctions seems astonishing in light of predictions based on the species-area relationship.

Puerto Rico's forests have been under assault over the past four hundred years, and early in the past century they were almost completely logged. Ariel Lugo, a researcher for the U.S. Department of Agriculture, concluded that only seven of the sixty bird species identified before the forest was cut down had disappeared. And today Puerto Rico has ninety-seven bird species, which means that while some went extinct others apparently flew in from other islands. Many species survived because the logging didn't result in bare land but rather in regrowth of the forest.

Although these reports give reason for optimism, they do not necessarily encourage complacency. Simon Stuart, head of the IUCN's Species Survival Programme, summarizes the views of many researchers when he says, "No one knows exactly what the current extinction rate is, but recent calculations by leading scientists put it at between 1,000 and 10,000 times greater than it would naturally be."[14]

Conclusion

Scientists do not know how many species are being lost each year. It is clear, however, that human actions increase extinction rates. But no one really knows whether we have a relatively manageable species-loss problem or a catastrophic one.

Part of the scientific method is to draw conclusions about the future based on available information and theories about what the

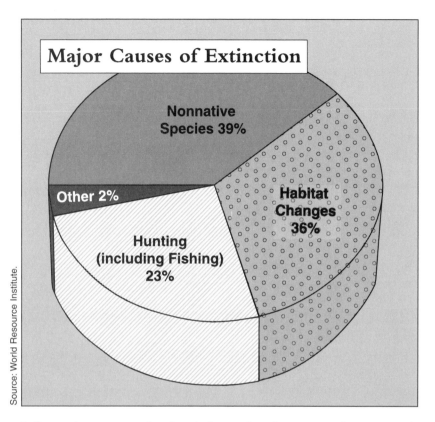

Major Causes of Extinction

Nonnative Species 39%

Other 2%

Habitat Changes 36%

Hunting (including Fishing) 23%

Source: World Resource Institute.

information means. As that information improves, changes, or is modified, the conclusions about the future can be changed. Researchers who make predictions about species losses do just that (revise their predictions as information changes), but a great deal of disagreement—and plenty of uncertainty—exists over method.

CHAPTER 2

Does the U.S. Endangered Species Act Save Species?

The recovery of the American peregrine falcon is a success story. Only thirty-nine known pairs of wild peregrine falcons—a large bird of prey—were found in the United States in 1970, and now more than one thousand pairs live in the lower forty-eight states, some nesting on skyscrapers in our largest cities. The bird has been officially designated by the U.S. government as recovered: A bird has been brought back from the brink of extinction.

Such restoration of endangered animals and plant species is the goal of the Endangered Species Act, a law passed by the U.S. Congress in 1973. Yet the act may not have had much to do with the return of the peregrine falcon. How successful the law has been is a subject of great debate.

The United States has been a world leader in creating legislation to protect endangered species. Canada has considered enacting a law similar to it. The European Union adopted the Habitats Directive, a law patterned after it, in 1992, in hope of saving some of Europe's most endangered species and habitats. The U.S. government also works with other nations' governments to protect species through an agreement known as CITES (the Convention for International Trade in Endangered Species). Its goal is to enable nations to act jointly in protecting species so that efforts by one country are not overridden by others.

According to M. Lynne Corn and other staff members of the Congressional Research Service, the Endangered Species Act is "widely regarded by its proponents as one of this country's most important and powerful environmental laws."[15] One environmentalist said that the Endangered Species Act is "not just our strongest environmental law, it's also a noble vision."[16]

Because the act embodies the principle that all species should be saved, it has been called "the most important environmental legislation the world has ever seen,"[17] and Americans have been instructed to "cherish and jealously protect the Endangered Species Act, the single most important environmental law ever passed by any society."[18]

Others, however, see the Endangered Species Act quite differently. Some focus on its rules and regulations and the harm they may be doing by making it difficult for people to conduct normal activities.

Nearly extinct in 1970, the graceful peregrine falcon has made a successful comeback in the wild. The role of the Endangered Species Act in this comeback is a subject of debate.

Former Senate majority leader Trent Lott complains, "They've tied up 100,000 acres in Mississippi for seven red-cockaded woodpeckers," and adds, "There's some insanity at work here."[19] Others view the law as unrealistic. Norman Christenson, a Duke University ecologist, says that "species populations fluctuate constantly. Species may go locally extinct in a given area. They may appear and reappear."[20] Yet the law is based on the idea that species, subspecies, and distinct populations should remain in their habitat forever.

The Endangered Species Act has been in effect for nearly thirty years. This should give enough of a track record to determine whether it has been effective in saving species. Does it bring them back from near extinction and is it the most important environmental legislation ever passed? Or, as some argue, has it been poor policy—raising hopes but dashing them as well?

The Goals of the Endangered Species Act

The stated goal of the Endangered Species Act is to protect all species, subspecies, and populations that face extinction and return them to a nonendangered status. To achieve this goal, government officials decide whether to list species as endangered or threatened. An endangered species is "any species which is in danger of extinction throughout all or a significant portion of its range."[21] (A plant or animal range is the area that the species at one time occupied; species identified as pests are exempted.) A threatened species is one that is likely to become endangered. The law also protects subspecies and distinct populations, so that a species that is numerous in one geographical area can be listed if it is about to disappear somewhere else.

The Endangered Species Act has been called "one of this country's most important and powerful environmental laws."

Once a species is listed as threatened or endangered, its habitat—the land or water in which it can survive—comes under the control of the Endangered Species Act. In most cases, this means that the

*Trent Lott,
Republican senator
from Mississippi. Lott
called the effects of the
Endangered Species
Act in his state
"insanity."*

U.S. Fish and Wildlife Service, an agency of the Department of the Interior, is responsible for it. In the case of ocean mammals and fish, the secretary of commerce, acting through the National Marine Fisheries Service, is responsible.

These agencies are supposed to see that no one can "harass, harm, pursue, hunt, shoot, wound, kill, trap, capture, or collect an endangered species." The law applies to both private landowners and public agencies. The law also prohibits people from selling or transporting any members of the species and from disturbing the species' habitat, if the disruption will harm it. There are severe penalties, both civil and criminal, for anyone convicted of actions that lead to the death of a listed species.

Does the Act Save Species?

Deciding whether the Endangered Species Act saves species is a difficult challenge. Concrete evidence of successful recoveries—that is, evidence that endangered animals or plants are now in a healthy state—is rare. The peregrine falcon is unusual. But, perhaps a string of successful rescues may not be the way to judge the act.

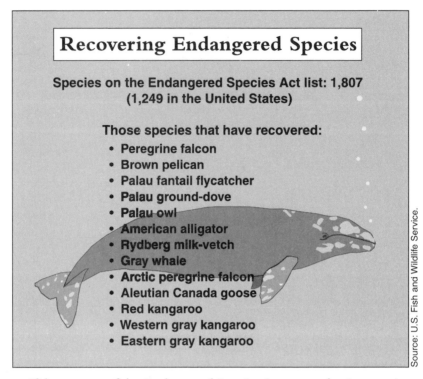

Recovering Endangered Species

Species on the Endangered Species Act list: 1,807
(1,249 in the United States)

Those species that have recovered:
- Peregrine falcon
- Brown pelican
- Palau fantail flycatcher
- Palau ground-dove
- Palau owl
- American alligator
- Rydberg milk-vetch
- Gray whale
- Arctic peregrine falcon
- Aleutian Canada goose
- Red kangaroo
- Western gray kangaroo
- Eastern gray kangaroo

Source: U.S. Fish and Wildlife Service.

If the success of the Endangered Species Act means having species recover to the point that they, like the peregrine falcon, no longer need to be protected by law, then the act is a failure. By mid-2001, only 13 species had been taken off the list due to recovery, and 7 species had become extinct since their listing (12 had been delisted for other reasons, primarily because new information indicated that they hadn't been close to extinction when they were listed). These changes are out of a total of 1,807 species (both plants and animals) listed as endangered or threatened. On this list, 1,249 species are found in the United States.

The species that have recovered, in addition to the peregrine falcon, are the brown pelican, Palau fantail flycatcher, Palau ground-dove, Palau owl, American alligator, Rydberg milk-vetch, gray whale, Arctic peregrine falcon, Aleutian Canada goose, red kangaroo, western gray kangaroo, and the eastern gray kangaroo. (Some of these are not found in North America, but they were listed in order to keep the United States from importing products made from their hides.)

The Endangered Species Act probably did little to save these recovered species, however. Most scientists believe that the principal cause of the pelican's decline was the pesticide DDT. This long-lasting chemical accumulated in the bodies of pelicans and thinned their eggshells, keeping many from reproducing. It was banned in the United States in 1972, and most experts think that the ban had much more to do with the pelican's recovery than did the Endangered Species Act.

Some of these "recovered" species may not have been facing extinction in the first place. The alligator was first protected in 1967 under legislation that predated the Endangered Species Act, but protection was based on data that were completely wrong. That is, the alligator was never in danger. This is also true for the Rydberg milk-vetch, a small flowering plant found in Utah's mountains. It was taken off the list when it was found to be more plentiful than originally thought. So, even though these species are officially listed as recovered, the term is a misnomer for them.

The peregrine falcon, like the brown pelican, apparently suffered because DDT had accumulated in fish and fish-eating birds. But it took more than a ban on DDT to bring the falcon back. A painstaking effort by Tom Cade, a Cornell University ornithologist, or bird

A brown pelican alights on the water. The ban on the use of DDT is credited with the pelican's recovery from near extinction.

expert, required years of breeding falcons in captivity. Cade had to combine modern science with the technique of falconry known as hacking. In the Middle Ages, falconers trained birds to become messengers; Cade trained birds to fly so they could live in the wild.

Another way to measure the success of the Endangered Species Act is to decide whether species, even if they are listed as endangered or threatened, are increasing in population numbers. That would be a sign of improving health. But a study by Environmental Defense found that "less than a tenth of all listed species"[22] monitored by the U.S. Fish and Wildlife Service were improving their status. Many more were declining in number, and for one-third, the status was unknown.

Of the species found exclusively on federal land, only 18 percent were improving, the report said. Of those found just on private land, only 3 percent showed improvement. And, according to the report, "even the low number included in the 'improving' category represents a stretch, for the category includes several species whose progress has been modest at best."[23]

What Standard of Success?

Recovery and improvement may, however, be the wrong expectations for the Endangered Species Act. Most species are listed only after they are well on the way to extinction. Reversing all the causes of decline takes time, perhaps much longer than three decades. "If you look at it in terms of preventing extinctions and getting species to a point where at least there is a chance to bring them back, then on that level it's been effective,"[24] says Christopher Williams, senior program officer for wildlife conservation policy with the World Wildlife Fund.

Another reason not to expect too much from the act is that Congress does not allocate large amounts of money to endangered species programs. According to the Fish and Wildlife Service, $348 million was spent in 1995, the last year for which the agency's data have been organized in a way that totals endangered species spending. "It's important to put this in some perspective. In the great scheme of what the government spends [$348 million] is not that great [an] amount of money," said Fish and Wildlife Service spokesperson Hugh Vickery. "It costs $40 million to create one mile of federal highway."[25] One environmental writer says that expecting "dismally underfunded" recovery programs to repair "the damage of centuries"[26] in just a few decades may be asking too much.

Another defense of the law is that only seven species listed as threatened or endangered actually became extinct. Some argue that this small number over nearly thirty years can be viewed as a success. According to the late Mollie Beattie, former director of the U.S. Fish and Wildlife Service, "Preventing extinction is our first goal. From there, we can begin to bring these species back to the point where they are no longer endangered."[27] Charles Mann and Mark Plummer, authors of a book about endangered species, observe: "Because many species are rare or limited to small territories, they may be so extinction-prone as to be virtually unrecoverable, at least by Fish and Wildlife."[28]

Shoot, Shovel, and Shut Up?

There is a reason other than inadequate funding that may explain the limited success of the Endangered Species Act. The act may encourage people to do just the opposite of what Congress wants them to do.

When an endangered or threatened species is found on someone's property, the Fish and Wildlife Service can take many powerful actions. Property owners can be prohibited from cutting trees, clearing brush, and using pesticides. Owners (both private and public) are often required to set aside acres to provide habitat for the endangered species. They can be prevented from planting crops, building homes, protecting their livestock from predators (if the predators, such as grizzly bears, are threatened or endangered), and building roads. In some cases, landowners cannot even plow a firebreak around their home to keep wildfires away. Thus, the government can prohibit people from using their land for making a living by normal activities, as long as government wildlife officials think that will protect habitat.

This can be costly for some, and it appears that some prop-

Congress does not allocate large amounts of money to endangered species programs.

erty owners quietly disobey the rules in ways that are not good for endangered species. Authors of an Environmental Defense study explain why: "They are afraid that if they take actions that attract new endangered species to their land or increase the populations of the endangered species that are already there, their 'reward' for doing so will be more regulatory restriction on the use of their property."[29]

If this report is correct, the Endangered Species Act is encouraging at least some landowners to destroy habitat. In fact, sometimes rumors surface that property owners "shoot, shovel, and shut up" if they find an endangered species on their property. That is, they quietly destroy the plant or animal and hope no one ever finds out. No one is sure that this actually happens, but tales abound. And certainly some owners take steps to keep endangered animals from settling on their property. For example, to keep the red-cockaded woodpecker off one's land, all one really needs to do is cut down trees before they get old enough to be attractive to the woodpeckers for their nests. Robert J. Smith, an environmental analyst, says: "The incentives are all wrong. The

The presence on private land of endangered species like this red-cockaded woodpecker can prevent the landowner from using the land so as not to violate the endangered species laws.

more wildlife habitat that a landowner leaves on his land, the more likely it is that he's going to be prevented from using his own land."[30]

As a result, the restrictions caused by the Endangered Species Act have some negative impacts on people. These effects may thwart the goals of protecting species and populations. By making it difficult or impossible to farm or build a home, the government may be deterring landowners from keeping endangered species on their property. Larry McKinney of the Texas Parks and Wildlife Department has said that "more habitat for the black-capped vireo, and especially the golden-cheeked warbler, has been lost in those areas of Texas since the listing of these birds than would have been lost without the Endangered Species Act at all."[31] In his view, people are trying to keep the birds off their property in order to keep out the federal government.

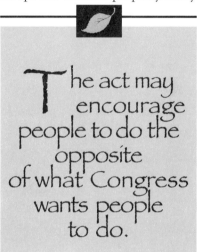

The act may encourage people to do the opposite of what Congress wants people to do.

A biologist at the Balcones Canyonlands National Wildlife Refuge in Texas supports McKinney's analysis. According to Deborah Holle, "If you do something to attract those birds to your property and then want to raise goats or sell your property, Fish and Wildlife will say you can't do anything now. The way it is, it would be kind of silly to help the birds out. The [ranchers] have to be realistic."[32]

There may be another reason why the act isn't more successful: Spending priorities may be out of line. Don Coursey, an economist at the University of Chicago, discovered some years ago that the agency spends much more money on large, dramatic animals, primarily mammals and birds along with a few reptiles (sometimes called charismatic megafauna), than on small and less attractive animals such as snails and insects.

Coursey conducted a survey to determine what the American public thought the endangered species budget should be spent on, and, indeed, the public wanted the bigger, well-known animals to be protected. So the Fish and Wildlife Service was doing what the public

Larger, well-known animals like this crocodile often get priority in preservation efforts over smaller, less appealing animals.

wanted—spending its funds on the animals that the American public wants to protect, such as grizzly bears, crocodiles, and wolves. Only a small portion of the agency's expenditures go for the Stephens kangaroo rat or the flower-loving Delhi swamp fly, little-known animals that people don't care much about. Says Environmental Defense attorney Michael J. Bean: "These tend to be species that are not well known and are not the focus of politically contentious controversies. They get put on the bottom of the heap, and little or no effort is put into recovering them. That's unfortunate because with a modest amount of money, recovery in the near term is an attainable goal."[33]

The Fish and Wildlife Service does not totally ignore these obscure creatures. Instead, it relies on private landowners to save them. Yet being forced to take costly steps to protect unpopular animals like insects and rats can make landowners angry. It may even lead to the "shoot, shovel, and shut up" phenomenon or, more likely, to efforts to keep out the endangered animals. These actions may help explain why the lists of endangered and threatened species keep getting longer in the face of thirty years of legislation.

Federal Programs

Only part of the Endangered Species Act is directed at private landowners. The act also requires federal and state programs to take account of endangered and threatened species. Before making large changes like building dams or government facilities, the agencies are required to determine the impact on listed species. In some cases, such as the Tellico Dam project in Tennessee and the Mount Graham telescope in Arizona, major projects have been delayed or modified because of a fish or squirrel.

Yet other federal programs are hurting endangered species. Jeff Opperman, of the University of California at Berkeley, found that 58 percent of listed species are at least partly threatened by federal activities. One of these activities is the Fish and Wildlife Service's own program to control damage by pests.

In the past, this program poisoned prairie dogs, which harm farmers' fields by creating prairie dog towns that interfere with crop growing and cattle grazing. These prairie dogs are viewed as pests. In addition to federal poisoning programs, many western and midwestern state governments have—at least until recently—allowed or even required eradication of the prairie dog. In some counties, if you did not poison off your prairie dogs, pest-control agents would do it for you, then make you pay for their work. The Utah prairie dog was almost poisoned into extinction.

The black-footed ferret almost disappeared, too. It feeds on the dwindling number of prairie dogs and even lives in prairie dog burrows. Black-footed ferrets were thought to be extinct by 1972, but a

In the early 1970s, the black-footed ferret, shown here, was thought to be extinct until a small colony was discovered in Wyoming in 1981.

small colony was discovered by a dog on a Wyoming ranch in 1981. Only when the dog brought his kill to his owner was this last population discovered.

Agricultural subsidies also cause species to slide toward extinction. According to Opperman, government funds to support agriculture have a detrimental effect on 332 species, making subsidies second only to urbanization in harming species (by his count, the growth of cities is threatening 336 species). Potentially harmful practices include converting habitat to farmland, which may involve draining land and fragmenting wildlife habitat; degrading water quality by allowing runoff of fertilizer and other chemicals; and allowing cattle to graze at the edges of streams.

So, while it may be too strong an assessment to call the Endangered Species Act a failure, a lukewarm success is probably the most that can be said for it. The act lists species but recovers almost none. Despite its goals, it is inadequately funded, poorly implemented, and often ineffective. It penalizes landowners and discourages conservation.

Policy Symbolism

Some critics of endangered species legislation think that the act was never designed to save species, but was merely symbolic. They argue that when it was passed in 1973, Congress did not even intend to accomplish its goals. Instead, the act was meant to reassure the public that something was being done about endangered species.

This view of a law is a highly negative one, and not everyone views politics as more symbolic than real. However, political scientists recognize that there are understandable reasons for engaging in such symbolism. Such laws may "placate idealistic environmental groups and a superficially informed public,"[34] says Michael Lyons, a political scientist at Utah State University. G.C. Bryner, another political scientist, points out that "dramatic promises" are often embodied in legislation because they arouse more "enthusiastic support"[35] than do minor laws that make minimal, step-by-step changes. If the promises are not realized, Congress can—and sometimes does—place blame on the bureaucracy charged with carrying out the law.

Indeed, the Endangered Species Act fits these descriptions. It contains ambitious goals. It is underfunded. It charges the agencies involved to save every species, even though that is an impossible assignment. Michael Lyons claims it is good politics but ineffective policy, and that it was designed to be just that. If he is correct, there is little wonder that evidence for the act's success is meager.

Conclusion

The Endangered Species Act is both extremely powerful and extremely weak—at least when measured against the high hopes that the public held for it when the act was passed in 1973. Yet it may be accomplishing as much as can be expected, given the challenge of protecting hundreds of at-risk plant and animal populations. The law lacks the extensive funding that would be required to save all the species that have been listed, and its penalties have discouraged some people from working cooperatively with government officials.

CHAPTER 3

Species Versus People?

The frog featured in Mark Twain's famous short story, "The Celebrated Jumping Frog of Calaveras County," was probably a California red-legged frog. When the tale was published in 1865, the red-legged frog was the most widespread amphibian in the state. But even then it was beginning to suffer from the ills that can send a species into a downward spiral—overhunting, changes in habitat, and the introduction of nonnative species.

Frog legs were considered a delicacy even in the nineteenth century; as a result, the frog was hunted for food. In addition, the frog's habitat was dwindling. The California gold rush of 1849 had brought miners to the state. Their excavations allowed streams to fill in with silt and dirt, reducing the clean-running water where the frogs thrived. Finally, at the end of the century, as red-legged frogs became hard to find, someone introduced the bullfrog to California. The bullfrog preys on the smaller red-legged frog. The three major causes of extinction—hunting, habitat change, and the introduction of a nonnative species—have all helped send the frog toward extinction.

In March 2001, the U.S. Fish and Wildlife Service took action to protect the frog. It set aside more than 4 million acres in California as habitat—an area about the size of Connecticut and Delaware combined. Landowners within those 4 million acres who need a federal permit, such as a Clean Water Act permit for a construction project, must prove that they will not harm the frog or its habitat.

"We think it's an important victory for the red-legged frog and the declining amphibian population in California,"[36] says a representative of an environmental group, the Center for Biological Diversity, which had been promoting the frog's protection. Not everyone is so enthusiastic. California is a fast-growing state and many people want to live there. Housing around San Francisco Bay is already among the most expensive in the country, and many new arrivals find it hard to afford a home. The ruling is likely to slow down home building and other construction, making it more difficult to find a place to live. A spokesperson for the Home Builders Association of Northern California said the ruling has the "potential to prevent this region from addressing its existing housing emergency."[37]

Two red-legged frogs hang on to each other in the reeds. This species faced extinction, but a 2001 law protected its California habitat.

These reactions reflect very different visions of what should be done about endangered species. At issue is a conflict between humans and species. To the Center for Biological Diversity, humans have been winning the conflict by introducing nonnative species, destroying habitat, and overhunting. It's time to start siding with the species, they say.

In contrast, the home builders think that plants and animals are the victors, and it's time to pay attention to people. According to this view, people are the endangered species.

Certainly, people have experienced losses because animals and plants have been protected. Consider the following:

Margaret Rector bought land near Austin, Texas, thirty or so years ago. Her hope was to have an investment for her retirement years. But she was eighty years old when the U.S. Fish and Wildlife Service decided that her fifteen acres are critical habitat for the golden-cheeked warbler. She was unable to build on it as she had intended. The value of her fifteen acres fell from nearly $1 million to just $30,000.

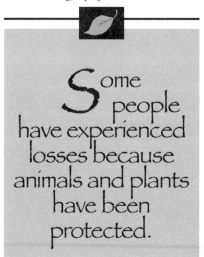

Some people have experienced losses because animals and plants have been protected.

Ben Cone had a parcel of seventy-two hundred acres of forest land in North Carolina. He liked having the forest, with its tall trees, for hunting quail and wild turkey. Periodically he cut down some of his trees to earn some money. But his land has red-cockaded woodpeckers. To protect them, the Fish and Wildlife Service put strict regulations on where he could log trees. Out of his seventy-two hundred acres, more than fifteen hundred were under the control of the government.

Yshmael Garcia owned a house in Riverside County, California, an area inhabited by the Stephens kangaroo rat, which is protected under the Endangered Species Act. The Fish and Wildlife Service told Garcia that he could not create a firebreak around his home by discing (that is, breaking up the soil with a plow). All he could do was mow the lawn. Unfortunately, when fires developed in October 1993, his home and twenty-eight others were destroyed.

John Shuler is a Montana rancher. Several grizzly bears had been killing his sheep, and one night a bear went after him as well. Shuler shot the bear, killing it. Even though Shuler was defending his life, a judge fined him $7,000 for killing an animal on the endangered species list. The judge said that Shuler put himself in danger and should not have gone after the bear. Nine years later, after a long process of appeals, the fine was dropped.

The Choctaw Nation Indian Hospital in Oklahoma provides health care for some of the poorest people in the United States. To reach the hospital, many must drive across the Sans Bois Mountains on narrow dirt roads, often only passable in four-wheel-drive vehicles, or take a forty-eight-mile detour over twisting country roads. In 1988 the Choctaw Nation proposed completing a thirteen-mile stretch of Highway 82 to eliminate the detour or the dirt roads. But the highway was not built because the proposed routes would have crossed habitat of the endangered American burying beetle.

The rules can even deter people who are motivated by a desire to help species. One such person is retired Montana State University professor of biology and genetics Dave Cameron. Cameron wanted to reintroduce a native fish to a stream on his Montana ranch. The Montana grayling had been missing from his region for many years,

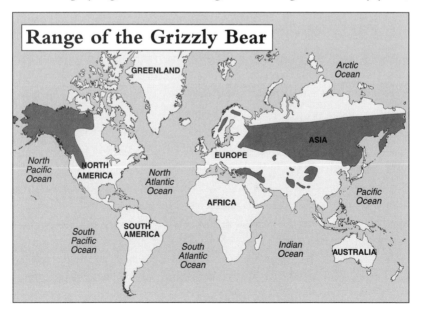

Range of the Grizzly Bear

possibly because nonnative fish were outcompeting it. Cameron found a suitable stream site on his property where he could restore the fish.

But then, says Cameron, "word arrived that the federal Wildlife Service was seriously considering listing the Montana grayling as an endangered species." At that point, friends who were familiar with government agencies advised him to forget it. Fearing that he might lose the right to graze his pastures, "I sadly bowed out," [38] he says.

Lose the right to graze his pastures? Yes. If the Montana grayling were listed as a threatened or endangered species, the Fish and Wildlife Service could take charge of the stream where the grayling lived. Officials could tell Cameron where he could and could not let his cattle graze because the livestock might disturb the water and endanger the grayling. Cameron felt quite capable of protecting the grayling and he didn't want government officials to tell him how to manage his ranch. By introducing the grayling, he could lose the right to manage his ranch as he saw fit.

Conflicts Around the World

These examples come from the United States, where the Endangered Species Act authorizes rules to protect endangered plants and animals. Although no other country, including Canada, has as tough a law, many other efforts are being made to protect animals in wild places around the world. These efforts also sometimes run into conflict with people's needs and desires.

Efforts to protect tigers in India, for example, may mean that those tigers will threaten livestock and children. In Africa, protected elephants may destroy a storehouse that holds a family's crop for an entire year.

Rules against killing some species can also hurt traditional economies. Strict international rules limit the number of whales that can be captured in the world's oceans. This means that Inuit whalers in Alaska, Canada, Russia, and Greenland come under the same rules as Japanese or Norwegian whalers. Not only are they poorer than the Japanese and Norwegian whalers, but killing and consuming whales is central to their cultures.

Protecting animals may mean setting aside land that people want to use for farming or other ways of earning a livelihood. The Maya Biosphere in Petén, the northernmost area of Guatemala, is supposed to be a preserve. But Maya Kekchi Indians, seeking homes, have built villages inside it. They are squatters. When Conservation International, an environmental organization, tried to get them to leave, a group of the settlers kidnapped thirteen of the organization's employees and burned their research station to the ground. In another incident a large group of armed squatters took forty government officials hostage when the government tried to evict the squatters. The hostages were released after the government promised to let the seven hundred peasant families stay. "We know this is an area for the animals and for the reserve, but there is nowhere else to move," [39] says Marcelino Tista, a resident of the region.

Many dedicated environmentalists have come to recognize that involvement by local people is essential, especially in poor countries. Where people are struggling simply to stay alive, they must have an incentive to protect endangered animals. Peter Jackson, a

Inuit hunters reel in their prey—a beluga whale. A traditional prey species for native peoples of cold northern climates, whales are protected by international law.

Asian tigers roughhouse in the wild. Dangerous as well as endangered, tigers may be unable to peacefully coexist with humans.

leading figure in the effort to preserve wild tigers in Asia, says that "ultimately, the tiger will only live on if people are willing to coexist with it. The tiger is potentially a danger to livestock and even to human lives. Effective management of tigers to minimize damage to human interests, along with wise behavior to avoid confrontation, is necessary."[40]

An Issue of Fairness?

Should the wishes of people be subordinated to the needs of animal and plant species? Many people struggle with this question.

To begin with, some people consider protecting plant and animal species a responsibility of humans that must be accepted. The Noah

Principle, a term adopted by biologist David Ehrenfeld, expresses this responsibility. In the biblical story, Noah gathered all the animals of the earth into a large boat, or ark, to save them during a flood that covered the earth. Noah saved every species. He did not ask which were the most important and he did not complain about what he had to do.

Not only is there widespread emotional support for saving species, but there is a strong scientific consensus that preserving species is valuable. Humans depend on a rich diversity of living species—known as biodiversity. Trees detoxify pollutants in the atmosphere, for example, maintaining the quality of the atmosphere and water. Tiny microbes decompose waste in the soil. Mangrove forests at the ocean's edge reduce flooding. Other forests reduce drought by absorbing rainfall and releasing it slowly into the environment.

When any of these species or populations become extinct, the areas they inhabit (their ecosystems) can become less resilient, less able to respond to shocks or gradual changes from storms, volcanoes, and other disruptions. As ecosystems become less rich in biodiversity, the species face less competition, becoming less genetically diverse and less able to respond to change.

There is a strong scientific consensus that preserving species is valuable.

Species are also an important source of scientific knowledge. Edward O. Wilson has estimated that if the information encoded in the DNA (the genetic material) of the common mouse were represented in ordinary-size letters, it would fill nearly all fifteen editions of the *Encyclopaedia Britannica* printed since 1768. Genetic information from plants and animals can be used as a blueprint for making chemicals and compounds. Aspirin, for example, is synthesized from salicylic acid, a natural chemical found in plants. Wild species of apples and other fruits may have desirable traits that can be bred into domesticated species.

Wild species are a resource that often go unrecognized for years. The cowpox virus was just an animal disease before Edward Jenner figured out that it could be used as a vaccine against smallpox. A penicillin mold merely made blue cheese until it was found to be the basis for the wonder drug penicillin. Even wild rubber trees seemed pointless before Charles Goodyear learned how to use their sap. "Yet the life of every American is profoundly different because of these species,"[41] says former New York senator James Buckley.

No one disputes the value of saving species, but not everyone thinks that humans must attempt to save every species, subspecies, or distinct population. "The law originally was conceived to help majestic animals, such as the bald eagle," writes David Hosansky. "But, to the exasperation of developers, it often is imposed instead to protect rodents and insects such as the Delhi fly and the Indiana bat—even though few people appear concerned about such species."[42]

Alexander Fleming in his laboratory. Fleming's discovery of penicillin, made from a common and, until then, unimportant mold has saved countless human lives.

Even if everyone agreed that the Noah Principle should be followed, that doesn't answer the question of who is to take on the task. Is preservation just the responsibility of those living and working where endangered species are found? Or is it a broader obligation that should be carried out collectively?

To many people, the answer is clear: Those whose actions are harming endangered species ought to stop taking those actions. They should simply obey the law. The act's broad powers are just another form of regulation, similar to the laws of a city. They are part of the responsibility one accepts when one becomes a landowner.

In this view, citizens have a duty to take care of endangered species, whatever the personal cost. Protection of plant and animal species that were using the land before the farmers, developers, or highway builders arrived is more important than the rights of the people who own the land now. Many fear that if the penalties were taken away, developers and companies would run rampant over endangered species. University of Arizona professor William Shaw worries that the "elimination of the Endangered Species Act would be like removing stop signs."[43]

But others argue that rather than penalizing landowners who ignore the Fish and Wildlife Service instructions, the government should reward those who do the right thing. If the government is unfairly taking advantage of those who harbor endangered species, then the government should persuade landowners to protect endangered species voluntarily, by paying the owners for helping endangered animals or plants.

So far, the courts haven't told the Fish and Wildlife Service that it has to pay owners, yet a number of critics of the law think that it ought to, both because it is fair and because it would provide landowners with an incentive to protect species.

The government already compensates people when it takes land for a highway or other public purpose, as the U.S. Constitution requires. If the Endangered Species Act takes away much of the value of someone's land, shouldn't the government compensate these property owners, too? Most of the property owners who are trying to change the act are not opposed to protecting species, they just want others to help pay the cost.

Many people oppose such a policy or even that way of thinking. "The whole idea that the government needs to pay people not to do bad things is ridiculous,"[44] says John Humbach, a professor of law at Pace University. On its website, the Massachusetts Sierra Club says: "Developers could bulldoze nesting beaches, factories could poison fish in lakes and rivers, and companies could chop down eagle nesting trees—unless we pay them not to."[45] In this view, such a policy would be unfair to the species and to the other Americans who want to see the species protected. Compensating landowners for obeying the rules to protect endangered species would be simply paying them to obey the law. The law is the law, they argue. Why can't we expect people to follow it?

Those who favor compensation respond that it is unfair for people to be penalized by restrictions on the use of their land, especially when many other people are free of such restrictions. The Endangered Species Act places burdens on some rather than others. And these burdens can be substantial. "By focusing the enormous power of the federal government on the supposed protection of rare species, the Act has made rare species unwanted and has even encouraged some people to get rid of them," says economist Richard L. Stroup. "This explains the paradox of the Act's enormous power and minimal results."[46]

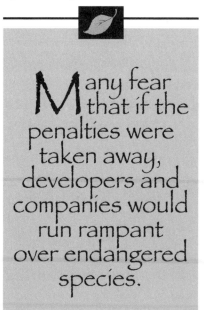

Many fear that if the penalties were taken away, developers and companies would run rampant over endangered species.

And these critics of today's law make an important distinction. They don't consider compensation the same as paying people to obey the law. Activities such as logging and home building are not normally illegal, they point out. Most people can do them. When the government prohibits some people from these activities, it is not because there is inherently something wrong with them. Rather, the landowners are being required to

A bald eagle swoops down on an unsuspecting fish. Protecting the eagle and other endangered species can place a high cost on some people.

do something extra beyond what Americans are normally required to do. This is different from prohibiting people from doing something that is wrong, such as causing erosion of other's property or polluting their neighbors' air. For such activities, people can be taken to court.

Most Americans live in cities and towns from which most endangered species have long since departed. Urban dwellers don't have to do anything themselves to protect endangered species. It is those who live near the endangered red-cockaded woodpeckers, northern spotted owls, and golden-cheeked warblers who must carry the burden. The cost to them can be quite heavy as they provide a benefit to others who do not have to bear any cost.

Tourists on safari in Africa enjoy the company of wild rhinos. Legally preventing natives from protecting themselves from large, dangerous animals may be unfair.

The Endangered Species Act, as it is currently implemented, illustrates a problem that the authors of the Constitution recognized: How much can the majority—in this case, those who enjoy the benefits of species protection—expect from a minority, those who are paying the costs? The founders of the United States instituted the Bill of Rights to keep the majority from taking away rights of others. The minority in this case are not racially or financially disadvantaged people; they are merely a smaller segment of the people than the majority. In this case, they are rural people who happen to have endangered species on their property.

The controversy is over whether the Endangered Species Act takes unfair advantage of these individuals. To help visualize this comparison, it might be appropriate to consider an analogy. Suppose that the government required people to take homeless pets into their homes. Is this comparable to what the government is demanding of rural landowners?

Some will say yes. But others will argue that the importance of endangered species in the wild is greater than that of homeless animals in the city, and therefore in most cases the burden is justified.

If the act is unfair—and that is what the debate is about—then forcing people outside the United States to take care of endangered species is probably more unfair. Few Americans have to worry about where their next meal will come from, but many villagers in Africa do. Should Americans—and other affluent people—expect villagers in Africa to live in fear of elephants just so Americans and other affluent people can know that elephants remain in the wild? Should Americans expect people to stay off land they want to farm because it is restricted for wild animals?

In Mozambique a farmer told a researcher from the National Geographic Society, "It's always the same. They say to us, 'You must share the land with wild animals,' but they end up kicking us out." His wife added, "The wild animals destroy our crops, and they kill people. Why should we share our land with them?"[47]

If others expect the species to be protected, they must find ways to deal with this apparent conflict. They may need to make endangered wildlife beneficial to the local people. *National Geographic's* Peter Godwin summarizes: "Most African wildlife lives outside actual game reserves, and unless local communities see direct economic benefits from wildlife, whether through ecotourism or hunting safaris, they will ultimately wipe it out."[48]

Conclusion

Political conflict occurs when one set of values is put into law and enforced through regulations. Those who favor the regulation are happy, but those who disagree with the set of values chosen are unhappy and try to change the laws and regulations. Today there is disagreement over whether endangered species protection, especially as followed by the Endangered Species Act but also by other countries' laws, is fair. This disagreement ensures that the conflict will continue into the future.

CHAPTER 4

Saving Species Around the World

The Endangered Species Act, which penalizes those who harm plants and animals in danger of extinction, is one way to attempt to save species. But others are being tried around the world. They can be divided into four categories.

First, some countries adopt a conservation reserve policy. The governments set aside large amounts of land for the protection of species and to keep local people out. Second, a "use it or lose it" policy protects species by making them valuable to local people through hunting, harvesting, or other uses; the species remain because they generate income. Third, ecotourism produces income by charging travelers for the opportunity to view wildlife and natural habitats. Fourth, captive breeding works to perpetuate captured species, either for release into the wild or to be sold for a profit.

These strategies can be used alone or in combination; each has strengths and weaknesses.

Conservation Reserves

Setting up a conservation reserve (or preserve)—a large area with biological diversity and sufficient space to allow animals to move around—and monitoring it to keep out poachers is a traditional way of protecting wildlife in peril. It may have begun in the United States in 1872 when Congress designated Yellowstone as the country's first national park and decreed that it should be kept in its natural state.

Essentially, a conservation reserve policy relies on keeping large amounts of land unused by humans and not allowing its wildlife to be used for meat, hides, or trophies. Such a policy is being used in Kenya to protect African elephants, in Indonesia to protect orangutans and tigers, and in many Latin American countries to protect endangered birds and butterflies.

Yet today it is one of the most controversial means of conservation. Such preserves often create conflicts with local people, who believe they should have access to land and wildlife.

An orangutan baby stays close to its mother. Orangutans are legally protected in their native Indonesia, a policy unpopular with some Indonesians.

In Africa, for example, preserves to protect the dwindling number of elephants in East Africa are not viewed as a success. Poaching (killing animals illegally) is rampant, partly because local people do not want elephants around them. They may cooperate with poachers. African newspapers regularly carry headlines such as "Elephants Invade Villages in Search of Food," or "Rogue Elephants Trample Three to Death." Elephants cause sleepless nights for farmers, who stay awake to chase elephants from their fields; a farmer "might wake up one morning to find his maize flattened and eaten, or his granary smashed and empty, his irrigation system destroyed, his harvest and his investment gone,"[49] writes Virginia Campbell for the World Wide Fund for Nature. No wonder that in a survey of peasant farmers, 97 percent strongly disliked elephants.

Farmers are unwilling to watch helplessly as elephants threaten their families and crops. Sixty percent of Africa's population consists of subsistence farmers, who may face a choice between killing an elephant or allowing it to live and themselves going hungry. For many poor, rural Africans, poaching can be a way to survive. A good pair of tusks may be worth four head of cattle, and the meat your family does not eat can be sold or traded to others. What is more, letting the elephant live may mean that it eats what little you have.

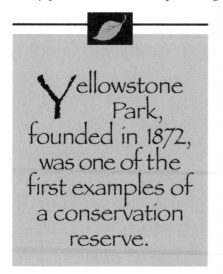

Yellowstone Park, founded in 1872, was one of the first examples of a conservation reserve.

Kenya and other countries in central Africa and East Africa, where hunting elephants and other wildlife is illegal, became a battleground in the 1980s as poachers killed elephants at an alarming rate and government officials responded by creating a "shoot on sight" policy. Armed park rangers shot anyone suspected of being a poacher immediately. In 1989, for example, Kenyan forces killed a suspected poacher every four days on average.

Kenya's government relied on setting aside about 6 percent of the country in national parks to protect elephants and other wildlife. The government made it illegal to sell ivory and sent armed guards after

A herd of African elephants ambles to the river. Although threatened with extinction, elephants are destructive and thus disliked by most African farmers.

people suspected of poaching. People who built villages inside the protected areas were driven out and their homes were destroyed so they would not return. Yet from 1979 to 1989, Kenya and other East African nations lost an estimated 77 percent of their elephants. In Kenya alone, the number was reported to have dropped from sixty-five thousand to just nineteen thousand during those ten years.

A Latin American example of a conservation reserve is Guatemala's Maya Biosphere Reserve. The region around it has experienced a population explosion, from about 25,000 people in the early 1960s to more than 300,000 by 1990. Population growth currently averages about 10 percent per year, an annual increase greater than the entire 1965 population, as people move from other regions.

The government, supported by environmental groups from other countries, wants to protect the area, which is a lush, tropical, lowland rain forest. Rodolfo Cardona, director of the National Council of Protected Areas, the government agency responsible for the reserve, says: "Put yourself in our place. You want us to go against a group of peasants who are victims of 400 years of repression. That is not possible." [50]

Relying on wildlife reserves poses several problems. The first is that local people often view parks as a threat to their traditional way of life and even to their survival. Why, they ask, should some of the best lands be reserved for animals when humans are barely surviving? They often respond by invading and settling the parks, as at the Maya Biosphere Reserve, or poaching the wildlife, as in Kenya.

A second problem is that reserves are simply not large enough to protect wildlife and still leave room for growing human populations. Even though 5 percent of sub-Saharan Africa has been designated as reserves, 80 percent of the continent's elephants live outside the boundaries.

A third problem is that protected wildlife populations can outgrow reserve areas. Elephant populations can increase by 5 percent each year and can destroy their habitat, to the detriment of all species living there. The best-known example is Tsavo National Park, one of Kenya's largest national parks, which covers approximately five thousand square miles. The park was created in 1948, when vegetation was so thick that elephants were visible only when they crossed a road. By 1959 elephants had become so numerous (around forty thousand) and their effects on the park vegetation so severe that the warden's wife described the park as a "lunar landscape."[51] They killed great boabab trees that were centuries old. A Landsat satellite image taken about twenty years later showed the park to be like a desert, with a thin scattering of live and dead shrubs and trees—"a wasted island amid a green land,"[52] according to one observer.

The mountains of Grand Teton National Park are mirrored in a lake. National parks in the United States have generally succeeded as wildlife preserves.

A bull elk trumpets its mating call. Thousands of elk starve to death periodically in U.S. national parks because their numbers have outgrown the food supply.

Some conservation reserves are successful, but they are primarily in wealthy countries where there are good alternatives to making a living in the reserve. Yellowstone National Park, Grand Teton National Park, and Rocky Mountain National Park in the United States do not have the kinds of problems that occur in less developed countries. People are not allowed to hunt there, but they have other lands for recreational hunting, and there is no pressure from squatters to live on the land.

Even these parks, however, can suffer from "Tsavo-like" problems. In Yellowstone, for example, biologist Charles Kay claims that the Yellowstone range is overpopulated by elk and bison. This results in the starvation of thousands of elk, an overgrazed range, the destruction of plant communities, the elimination of critical habitat, and a serious decline in biodiversity. Similar criticisms have been made of Rocky Mountain National Park in Colorado. Thus, simply setting land aside may not protect species as effectively as we think.

Use It or Lose It

In Zimbabwe and in other nations of southern Africa, a different approach has been tried. Their governments are preserving animal populations by allowing some of them to be hunted. For example, elephant meat is eaten and the hides are used for shoes, boots, luggage, and handbags. The hunters, who keep the ivory tusks, pay handsomely.

Zimbabwe and other countries in southern Africa allow villagers to manage wildlife that lives on the village lands. Zimbabwe's program is called the Communal Area Management Program for Indigenous Resources (CAMPFIRE). It involves the government, private nongovernmental organizations, and villages in "elephant country." Similar community-based programs exist in Mozambique, Zambia, Namibia, and Botswana.

Under CAMPFIRE, each season the local villagers determine how many elephants they will allow outsiders to hunt. They then sell the hunting rights to safari hunters. The money comes to the village, where citizens of each village determine how much of the income will be spent on community projects and how much will be kept by each household.

Masoka, an isolated CAMPFIRE community in Zimbabwe's Zambezi Valley, illustrates the impact. After five years under CAMPFIRE, Masoka's fields and settlements had new fences; wild animal attacks on people and crops had declined; children were being educated; local employment had increased; and household incomes had gone up. The citizens of Masoka now value wildlife in ways they never could without a program like CAMPFIRE.

These are called "use it or lose it" programs because people use and benefit from the resource—the animals or the habitat—that is being saved. The idea is that if there are no benefits, that resource will be lost and people will understandably interfere with conservation goals. They may poach on the animals (kill them illegally) or invade the reserve and claim its land.

In Guatemala's Maya Biosphere Reserve, the government and environmental groups are attempting to move from a reserve approach to a use-it-or-lose-it approach. They are setting up forestry concessions so towns outside the preserve can log nearby forests, leaving the preserve's forests alone. Another technique is to help small farmers outside the parks to obtain secure ownership of their property so they will be more likely to stay there instead of trying to plant crops on the preserve. And they are working with people who have settled inside the reserve and who have been allowed to stay, teaching them how to farm more effectively so they don't spread out further into the preserve.

Although use-it-or-lose-it programs seem to be working, they are far from perfect. In Guatemala, for example, some projects have failed. Sometimes local knowledge and traditions have been ignored. Locals worry that international environmental groups and their own government will not keep their promises and that government soldiers will move them out of their homes. Some residents continue the slash-and-burn agriculture that destroys forests.

Similarly, in southern Africa, multiple anxieties afflict the program. Villagers worry that existing programs will lead to Kenya-style national parks once wildlife populations reach high enough levels. Conservationists worry that the district governments will try to take control of the wildlife and keep money from the local villages.

And in Zimbabwe, the national government changed its policies, encouraging poor people to take over private land. This reversal was not directed at the CAMPFIRE program but it created enormous instability and alarm and damaged respect for the law. Poachers invaded one wildlife area, destroying fences and killing hundreds of animals.

Many conservationists are suspicious of the use-it-or-lose-it approach. "Using" wildlife is easily transformed in many people's minds to "exploiting" or "taking advantage" of it. The WildNet Africa website, for example, calls use-it-or-lose-it proposals "fallacies." The site, which is managed by a group of people who want to protect African wildlife, especially for tourism, notes that numerous animals have been "detrimentally over-utilized by commercial international

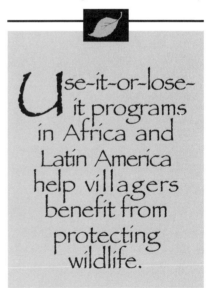

Use-it-or-lose-it programs in Africa and Latin America help villagers benefit from protecting wildlife.

trade,"[53] and recommends prohibitions against trade in ivory and other animal products.

Ecotourism

Ecotourism refers to tourism that benefits the ecology of an area. Its goal is to involve local people and to preserve the environment by attracting visitors who are interested in nature. It is quite different from the conservation reserve approach and has some similarity to the use-it-or-lose-it approach because it attempts to make the wildlife an asset to local people rather than a liability.

Ecotourism ranges from boat trips to see whales to photographic safaris through Africa's savannah lands. The WildNet Africa group calls ecotourism "the most notable alternative" for preserving wildlife, one that "provides a viable economic solution for uplifting local communities, which does not jeopardize their natural resources."[54]

Ecotourism is still young and no one is sure how effective it will be in protecting biodiversity over the long run. Can wildlife preserves attract enough tourists who want to see plants and animals in their natural state? And if so, does tourism require extensive hotels,

Tourists view native wildlife from afar. Ecotourism presents an approach to conservation that benefits both wildlife and local economies.

resorts, and facilities that may damage the environment the owners are hoping to preserve? Ed Sanders, former vice-chairman of the International Ecotourism Society, says that ecotourism should be viewed as one of many strategies to make conservation pay its way. Its goal is "to bring the value of wild habitat and wildlife up to the point where conservation can compete with other uses."[55]

One challenge facing ecotourism is to organize it in ways that actually help local people. Right now, in Kenya most ecotourism proceeds go to the cities from which tour companies operate, not to local villagers. At best, some local people are employed as guides, drivers, and hotel staff. A study in Tanzania showed that fewer ecotourism revenues went to local communities than revenues from sport hunting did.

Similar findings were made for preserves for the tiger in India. Many cater to tourists, but "tourist revenues in India make no significant contribution to either local communities or reserve management costs," says Michael 't Sas-Rolfes, a consultant on conservation. "Either tourists and tourist operators are not paying their fair share for the benefits they receive from tiger reserves, or their contributions are being misdirected (or both)."[56]

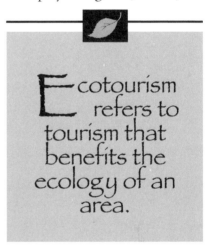

Ecotourism refers to tourism that benefits the ecology of an area.

Ecotourism seems to be working in some places, however. One example is the 260,000-acre Rio Bravo Conservation and Management Area (RBCMA) in Belize, Central America. Rio Bravo contains 392 species of birds, 200 tree species, 70 species of mammals, and 12 endangered animal species. The Nature Conservancy, the Massachusetts Audubon Society, Coca-Cola Foods, Inc., and a private foundation all have provided the funds for Programme for Belize. This private, nonprofit organization purchased the Rio Bravo property, which is 4 percent of the total area of Belize.

The Programme for Belize owns and manages the area under an agreement with the Belize government. Its financial goal for the long term is to have the area itself cover the costs of management, largely from ecotourism revenues. So, Rio Bravo has two field stations with educational centers and several ranger posts that host cultural and natural history tours. Tourists can visit Mayan ruins and picturesque towns. They can take part in rain forest and birding expeditions and hands-on archaeological and natural history research projects. So far, such projects cover 40 percent of management and protection costs for Rio Bravo. Other funds come from limited timber harvesting in the area and cultivation of thatch, palm, and chicle, the juice of the sapodilla tree that is a base for chewing gum.

Combined Strategies

Protecting endangered species may require multiple strategies. The Maquipucuna Reserve in Ecuador combines three approaches—use it or lose it, government-protected and privately protected reserves, and ecotourism.

Maquipucuna is an eleven-thousand-acre, privately owned and managed nature reserve surrounded by about thirty-five thousand acres of government-protected forest. Eighty percent of the entire area consists of steeply sloped, undisturbed cloud forest. This is high-elevation forest that is usually shrouded in clouds, where clinging plants, especially mosses and ferns, hang on to the trees. Biodiversity is rich because the reserve ranges from four thousand to nine thousand feet above sea level.

The Maquipucuna Foundation, which owns the reserve, hopes to create a corridor from high in the Andes to the coast to protect species that migrate between the highlands and the lowlands as seasons change. The main problem is an expanding human population that lives in the corridor the foundation wants to protect. Nearby, in unprotected corridors, people are cutting down the forest to create pastures for livestock. They burn the wood for charcoal, and kill and trap birds and mammals for food, for skins to sell, and for pets.

Maquipucuna wants to avoid such activities. To do this, it has purchased good lowland farms and traded them for highland farms in the cloud forest, which were ecologically more fragile and had lower levels of agricultural productivity. Ecotourism draws visitors to the highlands and generates income.

The foundation is also developing businesses that will keep the forests from being logged extensively. These include coffee plantations, including organic and shade plantations (which minimize the use of pesticides and fertilizers and use trees to keep the coffee plants out of the sun). Such protection produces higher-quality coffee, which commands a higher price. The foundation also produces organic brown sugar and preserves fruits. It makes paper from sources other than wood and uses bamboo instead of timber for building material. The foundation also receives funds from private organizations, foreign aid programs from various countries, the World Bank, and individual donors.

Captive Breeding

One of the more controversial strategies for preserving wild species is to breed them in captivity, either for release to the wild or to sell for a profit. This is controversial for two reasons. One is that captive breeding seems unnatural to some people, even if its goal is to return animals to the wild. It involves extensive human interference with nature.

The other reason is that many people feel that animal resources should not be used to benefit particular individuals, as they are when the animals are sold for profit. Rather, animals belong to humanity as a whole. Proponents of captive breeding respond that the profit motive may well be the only way to preserve the species or habitat.

The peregrine falcon was reintroduced to the wild by captive breeding by the Cornell Laboratory of Ornithology. Although there is some scientific debate over whether the released birds were "pure" enough to qualify as peregrine falcons, reintroduction would never have occurred without the decades-long study and experimentation at the laboratory. Similarly, black-footed ferrets were held in captivity to try to develop a large enough population to reintroduce them to the wild.

The more controversial use of captive breeding is to farm an endangered species for profit. The idea is that if the farmed animals, such as salmon or sea tur-

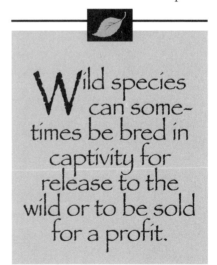

Wild species can sometimes be bred in captivity for release to the wild or to be sold for a profit.

tles, can be sold, there will be less pressure to hunt or harvest wild ones. Farming of salmon has worked reasonably well in the northwestern

United States, although it has also raised controversy. Some argue that farmed salmon may become genetically mixed with wild salmon.

Farming of sea turtles has run into problems from the laws designed to protect species. Sea turtles are found around the world. They live in the sea but lay their eggs on the beaches. Typically, the hatchlings run to the sea in a dramatic escape that can be breathtaking, and also dangerous because predators can pursue the hatchlings. But the major threat to the turtles are humans. Sea turtles are valued for meat, leather, and their shells. They are easily captured when the females come onto the beach to lay their eggs, and their eggs are easily retrieved. In addition, many former nesting beaches are now tourist beaches that have crowded out the turtles.

The Cayman Turtle Farm, located on Grand Cayman Island in the British West Indies, was created for captive breeding of the Kemps Ridley sea turtle. The owner wanted to produce turtles for the retail

A sea turtle deposits eggs in the sand. Sea turtles are vulnerable to hunters when on land to lay eggs.

Tourists play with young sea turtles raised on a farm in the Cayman Islands. International laws against selling turtle products have reduced the farm's profits.

trade as well as for release to the wild. The owner hoped to earn a profit while supplying farmed turtles. People would buy the farmed turtles and leave the wild ones alone. Or at least that was the idea.

However, the U.S. Fish and Wildlife Service does not allow sea turtle products to be sold in or shipped through the United States. This has shut off from the farm what might have been a major retail market. International trade in sea turtles is also prohibited by the Convention on International Trade in Endangered Species (CITES). The reasoning is that it might be impossible to distinguish between the farmed turtles and those taken from the wild.

In spite of these limitations, the Kemps Ridley turtle is still bred at the Cayman Turtle Farm and sold to the local market; the farm also has become a tourist stop for cruise ships. Together, vacationers and the local turtle market produce enough income to keep the farm operating but not at the commercial levels once envisioned.

Butterfly farming, a variation on captive breeding, is being tried in Kenya, as a way of protecting the Arabuko-Sokoke Forest. This largest remaining section of a once great coastal forest is rich in bird species. Ornithologists consider it one of the most important African forests for bird conservation.

It is so rich in wildlife that farmers who lived nearby at one time typically lost half their crops to baboons and elephants. As a result, they often raided the forest, cutting down trees in order to harm the species that depend on the trees.

The Kipepeo Project was created to enlist the local people in the protection of the forest (Kipepeo means "butterfly" in Swahili, and the project helps local people raise butterflies). Five hundred and fifty farmers are licensed to capture butterflies in the forest, take them home, and collect their eggs. After the eggs hatch, the farm-

Monarch butterflies gather to sip nectar. A butterfly farming project in Africa has succeeded in both saving the environment and providing a livelihood for local people.

ers raise the caterpillars on leaves gathered from the forest. Once a caterpillar forms a chrysalis, the Kipepeo Project purchases it and markets it to butterfly display houses and butterfly collectors in America and Europe. More than thirty-six thousand chrysalises are sold each year, and the farmers earn more from their butterflies than from all their other crops combined. They also now have an incentive to report poachers and illegal tree cutting to government authorities.

This breeding of butterflies has changed attitudes. Before the project began in 1993, 83 percent of the farmers living near the Arabuko-Sokoke wanted some of the forest cleared for farming, and more than half wanted all the trees removed. Today, just 16 percent want any of the forest cut. Butterflies, it turns out, are protecting the threatened and endangered species in the forest.

Conclusion

There is no "silver bullet" for saving species. Concerned people around the world are trying different approaches. They include establishing preserves, adapting "use-it-or-lose-it" programs, encouraging ecotourism, and conducting captive breeding.

CHAPTER 5

Facing the Future

The desire to save species remains strong, but multiple challenges lie ahead. Scientists, environmentalists, and policy makers debate how to save species. There is a great deal of soul-searching over how to involve local people in the effort.

One ongoing debate is whether people should even attempt to save all species. Edward O. Wilson says they should. He argues in his book *The Diversity of Life* that governments should have a commitment "to let no species knowingly die, to take all reasonable action to protect every species and race in perpetuity."[57] According to Wilson and others, to fully carry out the Endangered Species Act's mandate would require establishing huge areas as sanctuaries and stopping development of relatively undisturbed land.

Wilson suggests a way to do this. First, identify "hot spots," areas that contain large numbers of different species and that face a severe threat of habitat destruction. These hot spots should become protected reserves where no human development (houses, farms, or commercial buildings) is allowed. Wilson argues that the world's nature reserves, which currently represent 4.3 percent of the earth's land mass, need to be expanded to 10 percent of the land.

"Warm spots," areas less threatened or containing fewer species, would be zoned for partial development. Buildings could be constructed but only after taking into account the needs of the species found there. Remaining lands would be available for development but under restrictions.

Wilson's ambition is grandiose. He suggests designating the vast Pacific coastal area from southern Oregon to Baja California, known as the California floristic province, as a combination of hot and warm spots. This area contains one-quarter of all the plant species found in the United States and Canada. Half of the more than four thousand plant species found there occur nowhere else in the world. Yet this region is undergoing rapid urbanization and agricultural development, all of which limit available habitat.

Critics of Wilson's approach point out that although there is public support for preserves in relatively unpopulated areas, that support would disappear if populated areas as large as the California floristic province were off-limits. Although the United States has set aside many millions of acres as parks and wilderness, little of it is suited to urban living or even agriculture. Much of it would remain wild even if it had not been set aside.

Developing countries would face even greater opposition if such vast preserves were contemplated. Already, protecting parks and conservation areas from intruding populations and poachers is costly, and it may not be fair to the people who live around the parks. It is unlikely that millions of poor people will value hot spot preserves above their own survival.

Some analysts offer a much more restrained approach to saving species. Suzanne Winckler, a

"Hot Spots" are areas that contain large numbers of species and face a threat of habitat destruction.

freelance nature writer and employee of the Nature Conservancy, argues that "it makes little sense to rescue a handful of near-extinct species. A more effective strategy would focus on protecting ecosystems that support maximum biological diversity."[58] She suggests that endangered species should be protected the way that injured patients are treated in an emergency, a process called triage.

A whooping crane in its natural environment. Whoopers are endangered but have a high likelihood of recovery because their required habitat is plentiful.

In the case of medical triage, patients are divided into three groups—those who cannot be saved, those who will get well without much attention, and those who will survive only if they receive medical care. Medical attention is focused on the last group. In a similar way, Winckler recommends that governments and individuals spend money on saving only those species that have a good chance of surviving.

A triage approach would favor spending scarce resources to rescue the whooping crane. The reason is that there is sufficient habitat for the cranes, which spend winters at the Aransas National Wildlife Refuge in Texas and summers at their breeding grounds at Wood Buffalo National Park in Canada. Along their twenty-six-hundred-mile migration path, there are enough protected wetlands for them to stop over during the three-month journey. There are also captive breeding and reintroduction programs for whooping cranes at the Patuxent Wildlife Research Center in Maryland, the Calgary Zoo, and the International Crane Foundation in Wisconsin.

In contrast, heroic efforts to protect lynx populations in the northern Rocky Mountains would probably be rejected. The lynx has always been rare in the northern Rockies, which is the far southern edge of its historical range. A triage approach would not spend money on the Uncompahgre fritillary. This endangered butterfly is currently known to exist only in the high alpine meadows of the San Juan Mountains in southwestern Colorado. Scientists believe these butterflies thrived near the edges of glaciers ten thousand years ago. Today they are found only in small patches of habitat where glacier-like environments have persisted.

A triage approach reflects the fact that resources are scarce. It assumes that the nation cannot or will not act on the noble impulse to save every population, every subspecies, or even every species. It assumes that policy makers will have to make tough choices and, when making those choices, should rank their priorities.

Ecologists who take this position argue that when it comes to saving a habitat, all species, subspecies, and populations are not equal. Some are more important than others; the most important are called keystone species. The name comes from the construction of stone arches; if you pull out the keystone or center stone of the arch, the whole structure falls. A keystone species is one whose loss will completely alter an ecosystem.

Ecologist Robert Paine first used the term "keystone species" in the late 1960s. He studied the effect of removing a species of starfish from a rocky intertidal zone—the area between the high- and low-water marks of an ocean shore—in the Pacific Northwest. The starfish was the main predator of mussels. Once the starfish disappeared, the mix of intertidal species changed completely as the mussel dominated the zone.

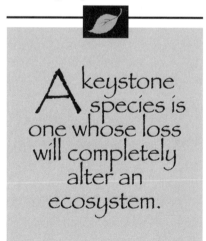

A keystone species is one whose loss will completely alter an ecosystem.

The beaver is an excellent example of a keystone species. When beavers move into a stream they immediately build a dam. They cut down trees for building materials, and their dams create ponds that trap sediment, resulting in a cleaner stream. Beaver ponds increase the area that is covered by water. Plant and animal species that once lived alongside the stream now have a much larger

This beaver dam creates a deep pond out of a stream and so creates a suitable habitat for many other species as well.

habitat. The ponds also raise the surrounding water table, changing the composition of plants and animals that thrive there. The beavers' dams change the flow of the stream, making it more consistent during the year, reducing the flow of water at its peak season and increasing low flows during summer.

Top carnivores—comparatively large animals that eat other animals and live at the top of the food chain—are often keystone species. The starfish is a top carnivore, for example. Duke University professor John Terborgh found that the big cats such as jaguar, puma, and ocelot in Central America have a major impact on their ecosystems. Where the cats are missing, herbivores (animals that eat vegetation only) dominate, completely changing the makeup of the plant species in the forests, including the trees.

Thus, keystone species tend to maintain a biological habitat over time and keep it full of diverse plants and animals. To maintain existing ecological habitats, protecting keystone species may be more important than protecting species with comparatively little effect on how ecosystems function. According to this argument, the most ecologically important species should be protected first—beavers ahead of spotted owls or jaguars ahead of butterflies.

Doing this would be difficult, however. Gardner Brown, an economist at the University of Washington, states the problem this way:

"We can't save every species out there, but we can save a lot of them if we want to, and save them in ways that make sense economically and scientifically. To do that, we have to make some choices about which species we are going to preserve. And nobody wants to do that! Nobody!"[59]

Triage has many critics. Whit Gibbons, senior research scientist with the University of Georgia's Savannah River Ecology Lab, for example, argues that it is wrong to give up on some species. All native species are worth the effort of saving. He says, "We must not put ourselves in the untenable position of ever having to consider eco-triage."[60]

New Ideas

Although scientists differ over how ambitious to be in saving species, the profession of ecology as a whole has become somewhat more optimistic about the ability of ecosystems that have lost species to recover. Ecologists today have changed their view of ecosystems as delicately balanced and unchangeable. Indeed, the "balance of nature" is a term rarely invoked by modern ecologists.

These experts are well ahead of the public, who was dramatically influenced by Rachel Carson's *Silent Spring,* published in 1962. Although her book targeted the dangers of pesticides, especially

This South American jaguar is an example of a keystone species. Without it, its habitat would change dramatically, thus affecting many other species, too.

DDT, it had a broader message as well. Carson believed that unless humans stopped upsetting the balance of nature by interfering with chemicals, many species would go extinct. The nation would be left with a silent spring, one without the birdsongs.

Carson's idea of the balance of nature reflected the views of most biologists at the time. Frederic Edward Clements, an early ecologist, had described the landscape as "a balance of nature, a steady-state condition maintained so long as every species remains in place."[61] The idea was that groups of species living together in a given habitat are organized into integrated communities, or ecosystems, and are highly dependent on one another.

In this view, ecosystems remain stable and balanced over time. Nature adds more individuals of one species and fewer of another, but the composition of species themselves remains largely the same. Rachel Carson claimed that it took "eons of time" for life to reach "a state of adjustment and balance with its surroundings."[62] Once balanced, this equilibrium presumably lasts more or less forever unless there is a major disturbance.

This perspective assumes that if a natural community is disturbed by natural events, such as fire or flood, or by human actions such as logging, grazing, or farming, a process called succession takes over when that disturbance ends. The area gradually returns to its original condition, including the original composition of species. The community follows an orderly process of one species replacing another until the system becomes a climax community—a stable and self-perpetuating collection of species. Therefore, natural systems will always return to climax conditions unless the disturbance upsets the balance of nature too much.

Yet the dominant thinking of ecologists has moved in the opposite direction. Most now believe that disturbance and change are better ways to describe the earth's ecological history. They emphasize that climate changes over time, glaciers advance and retreat, and the distribution of plants and animals contracts and expands. Local extinctions are a fact of life, as is the extinction of some entire species. Forest fires, floods, rising sea levels, the impacts of human activities, and general uncertainty are now seen as the norm in nature rather than the exception.

New species arrive, evolve, or leave when the ecosystem is disturbed and changed. Populations may disappear but the species may

A charred landscape is left in the wake of a large forest fire. Forest fires, though destructive, are now seen to be a natural part of earth's ecology.

live on elsewhere. Between disturbances, the system of relationships between the species that make up the ecosystem becomes more complex over time, but it doesn't form a unique ecological unit that will fall apart if a species leaves. Instead, it is essentially just a semi-random collection of individual species. If this is correct, then ecosystems are not delicately balanced or fragile. As long as keystone species remain in the system, losing one species or adding another will not cause major disruptions.

How to Save Species

These changing perceptions among scientists may give comfort to some because they suggest that some regions and species are more resilient than once thought. But that doesn't contradict the evidence that some animal species are on the brink of dangerous declines. Today, people around the world are more active than ever trying to protect species, whether tigers or salmon or elephants or wolves.

More and more, environmentalists recognize that the incentives of people who live with or near endangered species have a critical role. "Until recently, conservationists have skirted some of the key issues," says Michael 't Sas-Rolfes. "They have relied excessively on emotional media campaigns for public support and money, backed up by strings of regulatory measures that are poorly enforced and poorly funded. Fortunately, some environmental groups are redirecting their attention to the role of incentives."[63]

Incentives are the rewards and penalties that people expect when they take actions. In daily life, incentives guide everyone's behavior. People dress neatly because they know that employers and customers will treat them better than if they wear torn-up blue jeans and ragged shirts. People speak politely because the reward is usually a smile in return. People work long hours because their pay or promotion chances will be higher than if they do the minimum. All these are examples of positive incentives. (There are negative incentives, too. Drivers stick to the speed limit because they know they might get a ticket or lose their driver's license.)

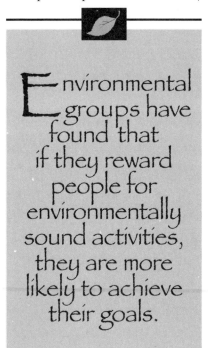

Environmental groups have found that if they reward people for environmentally sound activities, they are more likely to achieve their goals. As a result, they have begun using compensation or payments to obtain protection.

For example, the North Atlantic Salmon Fund is trying to protect the wild salmon in the waters of the northern Atlantic, including the ocean around Iceland and Greenland. Orri Vigfússon, an Icelandic businessman, organized the fund along with others concerned about the decline in the number of wild salmon.

During the past twenty years, the total catch of wild Atlantic salmon, worldwide, had been as high as 4 million fish; by 1998, the catch was just 800,000. Salmon were being overfished and could disappear almost entirely in that part of the world if nothing was done.

But something was done. Around Greenland, commercial fishers (that is, the fishers who haul in salmon and sell it) have legal rights to their catch of fish. If they fish there, no one else can. So the Salmon Fund bought these fishing rights owned by commercial fishers off Greenland and the Faroe Islands. Now the fund pays the fishers about $700,000 a year and helps retrain fishers for other jobs. Since the Salmon Fund bought the rights, no one else can fish commercially in those waters.

As a result of these purchases, twice as many salmon are returning to their spawning streams than before the compensation program was created. The fund receives its money from grants and donations from governments, interested organizations, fishing associations, and individuals concerned about the dwindling number of salmon. Some want to see the salmon return to streams and thrive so that they can fish them as a sport.

Defenders of Wildlife, an environmental group in the United States, also knows about incentives. The group wanted to restore wolves to the Rocky Mountain area, especially Yellowstone National Park. Wolves had been plentiful when the park was formed in 1872, but in the early years of the twentieth century, government agents and ranchers eliminated the wolves because they killed sheep and elk.

A wolf pack huddles together against the winter cold. Wolves have been reintroduced into Yellowstone National Park, where they once thrived.

Hank Fischer, a Rocky Mountain representative of the environmental group, wanted the federal government to restore wolves to Yellowstone. Yet he knew that ranchers feared the wolves because they kill sheep and calves. In the mid-1980s, he recognized that wolves were moving into the region naturally from Canada. Ranchers knew it, too.

How could he open the door to wolf reintroduction? He created the Defenders' Wolf Compensation Trust to reimburse ranchers when wolves killed their livestock. The trust has paid out about $175,000, compensating ranchers for hundreds of animals killed. By reducing the burden that had been placed on the ranchers, Defenders made the ranchers less opposed to having wolves in Yellowstone National Park and the region around it.

Wolves were restored to Yellowstone in 1995, and they thrived. Fischer had achieved the goal he had sought for a decade because he understood the role of incentives. "We try to make these programs as simple as possible," he says. "When I learn about a probable wolf kill, I typically call the livestock producer and talk. These are important conversations. Through these conversations I'm trying to bridge the gap between people who may not want wolves and my organization, which is committed to wolf restoration."[64]

Delta Waterfowl Foundation and Ducks Unlimited preserve thousands of acres of critical waterfowl habitat, using techniques that recognize people's incentives. Although waterfowl are not endangered now, some species once were. To keep the populations healthy, the Delta Waterfowl Foundation has an Adopt-a-Pothole program. Potholes in the northern United States and southern Canada are not the kind of potholes that one finds in highways; rather, they are depressions in farmland where water collects. These are perfect nesting places for ducks and geese.

Under the Adopt-a-Pothole program, the foundation pays farmers who maintain these as nesting areas rather than draining them to plant crops. And it pays farmers even more if they restore potholes that previously have been drained.

The Oregon Water Trust, a small environmental organization, also protects endangered fish and maintains the beauty of streams in Oregon by using compensation. It happens this way. In the drier parts of the state, ranchers and farmers often divert water from streams to

Preservation of natural beauty such as this region of Zimbabwe is definitely worthwhile, but agreeing on the best method to use in any given area is difficult.

irrigate their crops. This irrigation can turn the streams into a mere trickle that cannot sustain fish. So, the trust offers ranchers and farmers incentives to leave some water in streams rather than divert it for agriculture.

The compensation is not always extremely expensive. For example, one rancher stopped irrigating his pasture when the trust paid him enough money to buy the amount of hay that he had been growing for his cattle. The trust has also paid for technical improvements in irrigation so that a farmer will take less water from a stream. The trust is funded by private donors, corporations, foundations, and government agencies.

Compensation has led to significant success, but some people are leery of it. They criticize compensation along the same lines as some criticize the use-it-or-lose-it approach to conservation in Zimbabwe, or the idea of governments paying landowners to protect species under the Endangered Species Act.

Paying people to do what some argue is a duty to begin with does not sit well with a number of people, yet it may be inevitable. A few years ago, three environmental groups, the Greater Yellowstone Coalition, the World Wildlife Fund, and Environmental Defense, joined together to figure out ways to protect the special character of the region around Yellowstone National Park. They wrote that "the right mix of economic incentives can play a useful role in protecting agricultural lands and wildlife habitat in the Yellowstone region. No single approach will provide a complete solution to the problems associated with rapid growth and development. But some combination of the right incentives can help communities deal effectively with these problems."[65]

Some warn against too much reliance on such approaches, however. Environmental organizations that compensate fishers or ranchers rely heavily on donations. Are there enough dollars and enough interested people to make voluntary programs work for more than just a few species? The North Atlantic Salmon Fund spends about $700,000 per year to protect the North Atlantic salmon. The U.S. Fish and Wildlife Service spends about $36 million on Chinook salmon (a

These salmon benefit from millions of dollars spent by governments and organizations to preserve their habitat. Critics debate whether it is money well spent.

species of salmon) in the Snake River in the Pacific Northwest. Ironically, low levels of spending can be more effective than much higher spending levels by national governments. The Chinook salmon show no improvement, whereas Atlantic salmon do. Nevertheless, the difference in spending levels is striking.

Conclusion

As this chapter indicates, debates continue in the community of environmentalists and ecologists on many issues. Some assumptions that led to the design of laws such as the Endangered Species Act— the idea that every distinct population of a species must be actively protected and that nature is always in balance—are being questioned. These debates will continue; however, one emerging idea seems to be sticking: the idea that people must have incentives to protect species. Exactly how this idea will frame or shape endangered species protection in the years ahead is not fully known. All who are concerned about maintaining the species of today will want to watch closely as new experiments emerge.

 Notes

Introduction

1. David Quammen, "Planet of Weeds," *Harper's,* October 1998, p. 57.

Chapter 1: How Endangered Are the World's Species?

2. David Hosansky, "Mass Extinction," *CQ Researcher,* September 15, 2000, p. 713.

3. Bjørn Lomborg, *The Skeptical Environmentalist.* London: Cambridge University Press, 2000, p. 249.

4. Quammen, "Planet of Weeds," p. 67.

5. Quoted in K.A. Kohm, ed., *Balancing on the Brink of Extinction: The Endangered Species Act and Lessons for the Future.* Washington, DC: Island Press, 1991, p. 4.

6. Lomborg, *The Skeptical Environmentalist,* p. 257.

7. Edward O. Wilson, *The Diversity of Life.* Cambridge, MA: Harvard University Press, 1992, p. 280.

8. Quoted in W. Wayt Gibbs, "On the Termination of Species," *Scientific American,* November 2001, p. 43.

9. Julian L. Simon and Aaron Wildavsky, "Species Loss Revisited," in Julian L. Simon, ed., *The State of Humanity.* Cambridge, MA: Blackwell, 1995, p. 351.

10. Charles C. Mann and Mark L. Plummer, *Noah's Choice: The Future of Endangered Species.* New York: Alfred A. Knopf, 1995, p. 65.

11. Daniel S. Simberloff, "Experimental Zoogeography of Islands: Effects of Island Size," *Ecology,* July 1976, p. 629.

12. Quoted in Mann and Plummer, *Noah's Choice,* p. 95.

13. Gregg Easterbrook, "The Birds," *New Republic,* March 28, 1994, p. 29.

14. Simon Stuart, "Species: Unprecedented Extinction Rate, And It's Increasing." 2000. www.iucn.org.

Chapter 2: Does the U.S. Endangered Species Act Save Species?

15. M. Lynne Corn et al., "Endangered Species: Continuing Controversy," Congressional Research Service Issue Brief IB95003, 1995, p. 1.

16. Brock Evans, "The Endangered Species Coalition: From the Director." www.stopextinction.org.

17. G.B. Shaller, quoted in "The Case for Saving Species," *Defenders,* Summer 1995. www.defenders.org.

18. J.W. Fitzpatrick, quoted in "The Case for Saving Species," *Defenders,* Summer 1995. www.defenders.org.

19. Quoted in National Cattlemen's Beef Association, "Lott: ESA Needs Common-Sense Revisions," June 12, 2001. http://hill.beef.org.

20. Quoted in Monte Basgall, "Defining a New Ecology," *Duke Magazine,* May/June, 1996, p. 41.

21. *Endangered Species Act of 1973,* sec. 3 (6).

22. David S. Wilcove et al., "Rebuilding the Ark: Toward a More Effective Endangered Species Act for Private Land," December 5, 1996. www.edf.org.

23. Wilcove, "Rebuilding the Ark."

24. Hosansky, "Mass Extinction," p. 721.

25. B. Baker, "Spending on the Endangered Species Act—Too Much or Not Enough?" *BioScience,* April 1999, p. 279.

26. T.H. Watkins, "What's Wrong with the Endangered Species Act? Not Much and Here's Why," *Audubon,* January 1996, p. 40.

27. Quoted in Watkins, "What's Wrong with the Endangered Species Act?" p. 40.

28. Mann and Plummer, *Noah's Choice,* p. 246.

29. Wilcove, "Rebuilding the Ark."

30. Quoted in Hosansky, "Mass Extinction," p. 721.

31. Larry McKinney, "Reauthorizing the Endangered Species Act—Incentives for Rural Land Owners," in Wendy E. Hud-

son, ed., *Building Economic Incentives into the Endangered Species Act: A Special Report from Defenders of Wildlife.* Washington, DC: Defenders of Wildlife, 1994, p. 74.

32. Quoted in Mann and Plummer, *Noah's Choice,* p. 210.

33. Quoted in Baker, "Spending on the Endangered Species Act—Too Much or Not Enough?" p. 279.

34. Michael Lyons, "Political Self-Interest and U.S. Environmental Policy," *Natural Resources Journal,* Spring 1999, p. 271.

35. G.C. Bryner, *Bureaucratic Discretion: Law and Policy in Federal Regulatory Agencies.* New York: Pergamon Press, 1987, p. 207.

Chapter 3: Species Versus People?

36. Quoted in A. Kondo, "A Patchwork Habitat for Red-Legged Frog," *Los Angeles Times,* March 7, 2001, p. A3.

37. Quoted in Kondo, "A Patchwork Habitat for Red-Legged Frog," p. A3.

38. David Cameron, testimony at hearing of the House Committee on Resources, 104th Cong., 1st sess., May 25, 1995, p. 165.

39. Quoted in John Burnett, "Guatemala Struggles to Protect Rain Forest from Invaders," May 1998. www.planeta.com.

40. Peter Jackson, "A Future for Tigers," *People and the Planet,* no. 4, 1998. www.peopleandplanet.net.

41. Quoted in P.M. Hoose, *Building an Ark: Tools for the Preservation of Natural Diversity Through Land Protection.* Covelo, CA: Island Press, 1981, p. 1.

42. Hosansky, "Mass Extinction," p. 723.

43. Quoted in "The Case for Saving Species."

44. Quoted in D. Harbrecht, "A Question of Property Rights and Wrongs," *National Wildlife,* October/November 1994, p. 6.

45. Massachusetts Sierran Online, April/May 1999. www.sierra clubmass.org.

46. Richard L. Stroup, *The Endangered Species Act: Making Innocent Species the Enemy.* Bozeman, MT: Political Economy Research Center, April 1995, p. 4.

47. Quoted in Peter Godwin, "Without Borders: United Africa's Wildlife Reserves," *National Geographic,* September 2001, p. 12.

48. Peter Godwin, "Without Borders," p. 25.

Chapter 4: Saving Species Around the World

49. Virginia Campbell, "Elephants in the Balance: Conserving Africa's Elephants," World Wide Fund for Nature. www.panda.org.

50. Quoted in Burnett, "Guatemala Struggles to Protect Rain Forest from Invaders."

51. Daphne Sheldrick, *The Tsavo Story.* London: Collins and Harvill Press, 1973, p. 113.

52. Daniel B. Botkin, *Discordant Harmonies: A New Ecology for the Twenty-First Century.* New York: Oxford University Press, 1990, p. 16.

53. WildNet Africa, "The Case Against Commercial Trade in Elephant Products," 2001. http://wildnetafrica.co.za.

54. WildNet Africa, "The Case Against Commercial Trade in Elephant Products."

55. Telephone interview with Ed Sanders, Ecotourism International Society, September 2001.

56. Michael 't Sas-Rolfes, *Who Will Save the Wild Tiger?* Bozeman, MT: Political Economy Research Center, February 1998, p. 17.

Chapter 5: Facing the Future

57. Wilson, *The Diversity of Life,* p. 342.

58. Suzanne Winckler, "Stopgap Measure," *Atlantic Monthly,* January 1992, p. 74.

59. Quoted in Mann and Plummer, *Noah's Choice,* p. 66.

60. Whit Gibbons, "No Matter How Endangered, Every Species Should Be Protected," *Online Athens,* November 19, 2000. www.onlineathens.com.

61. Quoted in M.G. Barbour, "Ecological Fragmentation in the Fifties," in W. Cronin, ed., *Uncommon Ground: Toward Reinventing Nature.* New York: W.W. Norton, 1995, p. 235.

62. Rachel Carson, *Silent Spring.* Boston: Houghton Mifflin, 1962, p. 5.

63. 't Sas-Rolfes, *Who Will Save the Wild Tiger?* p. 23.

64. Hank Fischer, "Who Pays for Wolves?" *PERC Reports.* December 2001, p. 9.

65. Greater Yellowstone Coalition, World Wildlife Fund, and Environmental Defense Fund, *Incentives for Conserving Open Lands in Greater Yellowstone.* Bozeman, MT: Greater Yellowstone Coalition, 1998, p. 5.

 **Glossary**

distinct population: A population of animals or plants that has unique characteristics that differentiate it from other members of its species or subspecies.

ecosystem: An area that is studied for its interactions of species and the natural environment; it can be large or small.

endangered species: A species that is declining in number, possibly nearing the point of disappearing (extinction).

Endangered Species Act: A U.S. law enacted in 1973 that requires the federal government and individuals to take steps to protect endangered species.

extinction: Total disappearance of a species, subspecies, or distinct population.

fungi: Plants such as molds and mushrooms that have no chlorophyll.

habitat: The area in which a species lives.

keystone species: Species that have a disproportionately large effect on their community.

ornithologist: A scientist who studies birds.

slash-and-burn agriculture: Cutting down and then burning forests in order to make the land usable for farming.

species: The most basic biological classification; a group of plants or animals that are quite similar.

species-area relationship: A rule of thumb by which ecologists estimate the loss of species; in general, if 90 percent of a habitat is completely changed, the number of species is expected to decline by between 10 and 50 percent.

subspecies: A group that is slightly different from other groups in the same species.

For Further Reading

Books

Raymond Bonner, *At the Hand of Man: Peril and Hope for Africa's Wildlife*. New York: Alfred A. Knopf, 1993. Bonner, a *New York Times* reporter, takes a firsthand look at the controversy surrounding elephant protection in Africa.

Stephen Budiansky, *Nature's Keepers: The New Science of Nature Management*. New York: The Free Press, 1995. A discussion of biologists' changing attitudes about ecology.

Bjørn Lomborg, 2001. *The Skeptical Environmentalist*. London: Cambridge University Press. A professor and former member of the environmental group Greenpeace takes a critical look at claims that the environment is getting worse.

Charles C. Mann and Mark L. Plummer, *Noah's Choice: The Future of Endangered Species*. New York: Alfred A. Knopf, 1995. A thoughtful analysis of the full range of endangered species controversies.

Norman Myers, *The Sinking Ark: A New Look at the Problem of Disappearing Species*. Oxford: Pergamon Press, 1979. The book that started the debate over how many species are disappearing.

Edward O. Wilson, *The Diversity of Life*. Cambridge, MA: Belknap Press of Harvard University Press, 1992. An important biologist surveys the variety and richness of living things, explaining their past and warning about their future.

Periodicals

W. Wayt Gibbs, "On the Termination of Species," *Scientific American*, November 2001.

David Quammen, "Planet of Weeds," *Harper's*, October 1998.

T.H. Watkins, "What's Wrong with the Endangered Species Act? Not Much and Here's Why." *Audubon*, January 1996.

Suzanne Winckler, "Stopgap Measure," *Atlantic Monthly*, January 1992.

Internet Sites

Virginia Campbell, "Elephants in the Balance: Conserving Africa's Elephants," World Wide Fund for Nature. www.panda.org.

D.S. Wilcove et al., "Rebuilding the Ark: Toward a More Effective Endangered Species Act for Private Land," December 5, 1996. www.edf.org.

WildNet Africa, "The Case Against Commercial Trade in Elephant Products," 2001. http://wildnetafrica.co.za.

Works Consulted

Books

R.H.V. Bell and E. Mcshane-Caluzi, eds., *Conservation and Wildlife Management in Africa*. Proceedings: U.S. Peace Corps Workshop, Kasungu National Park Malawi, October 1984.

Daniel B. Botkin, *Discordant Harmonies: A New Ecology for the Twenty-First Century*. New York: Oxford University Press, 1990.

G.C. Bryner, *Bureaucratic Discretion: Law and Policy in Federal Regulatory Agencies*. New York: Pergamon Press, 1987.

Rachel Carson, *Silent Spring*. Boston: Houghton Mifflin, 1962.

Alston Chase, *In a Dark Wood: The Fight over Forests and the Rising Tyranny of Ecology*. Boston: Houghton Mifflin, 1995.

Alston Chase, *Playing God in Yellowstone: The Destruction of America's First National Park*. Boston: Atlantic Monthly Press, 1986.

N.M. Collins and J.A. Thomas, eds., *The Conservation of Insects and Their Habitats*. London: Academic Press, 1991.

D.G. Despain, ed., *Plants and Their Environments—Proceedings of the First Biennial Scientific Conference on the Greater Yellowstone Ecosystem*. Denver, CO: U.S. National Park Service, 1994.

Roger L. DiSilvestro, *Reclaiming the Last Wild Places: A New Agenda for Biodiversity*. New York: John Wiley and Sons, 1993.

David Ehrenfeld, *The Arrogance of Humanism*. Oxford, Oxford University Press, 1978.

P.R. Ehrlich and A.H. Ehrlich, *Extinction: The Cause and Consequences of the Disappearance of Species*. New York: Random House, 1981.

M. Fiorina, *Congress, Keystone of the Washington Establishment*. New Haven, CT: Yale University Press, 1997.

M.M.R. Freeman and Urs Kreuter, *Elephants and Whales: Resources for Whom?* Basel, Switzerland: Gordon and Breach, 1994.

P.M. Hoose, *Building an Ark: Tools for the Preservation of Natural Diversity Through Land Protection*. Covelo, CA: Island Press, 1981.

Wendy E. Hudson, ed., *Building Economic Incentives into the Endangered Species Act: A Special Report from Defenders of Wildlife.* Washington, DC: Defenders of Wildlife, 1994.

C. Hunter, ed., *The Life and Letters of Alexander Wilson.* Philadelphia: American Philosophical Society, 1983.

Ivory Trade Review Group, *The Ivory Trade and the Future of the African Elephant.* Vol. 1. Oxford: International Development Centre, 1989.

K.A. Kohm, ed., *Balancing on the Brink of Extinction: The Endangered Species Act and Lessons for the Future.* Washington, DC: Island Press, 1991.

Aldo Leopold, *A Sand County Almanac.* New York: Oxford University Press, 1949.

Bjørn Lomborg, *The Skeptical Environmentalist.* London: Cambridge University Press, 2000.

Charles C. Mann and Mark L. Plummer, *Noah's Choice: The Future of Endangered Species.* New York: Alfred A. Knopf, 1995.

Norman Myers, *The Sinking Ark: A New Look at the Problem of Disappearing Species.* Oxford: Pergamon Press, 1979.

B.G. Norton, *Why Preserve Natural Variety?* Princeton, NJ: Princeton University Press, 1987.

R.B. Primack et al., eds, *Timber, Tourists, and Temples: Conservation and Development in the Maya Forest of Belize, Guatemala, and Mexico.* Washington, DC: Island Press, 1998.

Daphne Sheldrick, *The Tsavo Story.* London: Collins and Harvill Press, 1973.

Julian L. Simon, ed., *The State of Humanity.* Cambridge, MA: Blackwell, 1995.

John Terborgh, *Diversity and the Tropical Rainforest.* New York: Scientific American Library, W.H. Freeman, 1992.

T.C. Whitmore and J.A. Sayer, eds., *Tropical Deforestation and Species Extinction.* London: Chapman & Hall, 1992.

D.S. Wilcove, *The Condor's Shadow: The Loss and Recovery of Wildlife in America.* New York: W.H. Freeman, 2000.

Bruce Yandle, ed., *Land Rights: The 1990s Property Rights Rebellion.* Lanham, MD: Rowman and Littlefield, 1995.

Periodicals

P.L. Angermeier and J.R. Karr, "Biological Integrity Versus Biological Diversity as Policy Directives," *BioScience*, November 1994.

B. Baker, "Spending on the Endangered Species Act—Too Much or Not Enough?" *BioScience*, April 1999.

A. Bingner, "Cayman Turtle Farm Suffers from Ban on Giant Green Sea Turtle Imports," *Aquaculture Magazine*, May/June 1981.

W.J. Boecklen and N.J. Gotelli, "Island Biogeographic Theory and Conservation Practice: Species-Area or Specious-Area Relationships?" *Biological Conservation*, May 1984.

D. Boroughs, "On the Wings of Hope: In Kenya, Butterflies Are Saving a Unique Coastal Forest and the Impoverished People Who Live There," *International Wildlife*, July/August 2000.

H.B. Britten, P.F. Brussard, and D.D. Murphy, "The Pending Extinction of the Uncompahgre Fritillary Butterfly," *Conservation Biology*, March 1994.

E.F. Connor, and E.D. McCoy, "The Statistics and Biology of the Species-Area Relationship," *American Naturalist*, June 1979.

W. Cronin, ed., *Uncommon Ground: Toward Reinventing Nature.* New York: W.W. Norton, 1995.

B. Czech, and P.R. Krausman, "The Species Concept, Species Prioritization, and the Technical Legitimacy of the Endangered Species Act," *Renewable Resources Journal*, Spring 1998.

Gregg Easterbrook, "The Birds," *New Republic*, March 28, 1994.

A. Easter-Pilcher, "Implementing the Endangered Species Act: Assessing the Listing of Species as Endangered or Threatened," *BioScience*, May 1996.

Paul R. Ehrlich and Edward O. Wilson, "Biodiversity Studies: Science and Policy," *Science*, August 16, 1991.

Hank Fischer, "Who Pays for Wolves?" *PERC Reports*, December 2001.

L. Fortmann, "Voices from Communities Managing Wildlife in Southern Africa," *Society & Natural Resources*, July 1997.

Peter Godwin, "Without Borders: Uniting Africa's Wildlife Reserves," *National Geographic*, September 2001.

D. Harbrecht, "A Question of Property Rights and Wrongs," *National Wildlife*, October/November 1994.

David Hosansky, "Mass Extinction," *CQ Researcher*, September 15, 2000.

Charles E. Kay, "Aboriginal Overkill and Native Burning: Implications for Modern Ecosystem Management," *Western Journal of Applied Forestry*, October 1995.

Charles E. Kay, "The Impact of Ungulates and Beaver on Riparian Communities in the Intermountain West," *Natural Resources and Environmental Issues*, vol. 1, 1994.

A. Kondo, "A Patchwork Habitat for Red-Legged Frog," *Los Angeles Times*, March 7, 2001.

Michael Lyons, "Political Self-Interest and U.S. Environmental Policy," *Natural Resources Journal*, Spring 1999.

L.S. Mills, M.E. Soulé, and D.F. Doak, "The Keystone-Species Concept in Ecology and Conservation," *BioScience*, April 1993.

R.F. Noss, "Building a Wilderness Recovery Network," *George Wright Forum*, Winter 1994.

R.F. Noss, "The Wildlands Project: Land Conservation Strategy," *Wild Earth*, Special Issue no. 1, 1992.

David Quammen, "Planet of Weeds," *Harper's*, October 1998.

A. Ricciardi, F.G. Whorisky, and J.B. Rasmussen, "Impact of *Dreissena* Infestation on Native Unionid Bivalves from *Dreissena* Field Density," *Canadian Journal of Fisheries and Aquatic Sciences*, June 1996.

Jonathan Rotter and Kyle Danish, "Forest Carbon and the Kyoto Protocol's Clean Development Mechanism," *Journal of Forestry*, May 2000.

Roger A. Sedjo, "Preserving Biodiversity as a Resource," *Resources*, Winter 1992.

Daniel S. Simberloff, "Experimental Zoogeography of Islands: Effects of Island Size," *Ecology*, July 1976.

D.W. Steadman, "Extinction of Birds in Eastern Polynesia: A Review of the Record, and Comparisons with Other Pacific Island Groups," *Journal of Archaeological Science*, March 1989.

Richard L. Stroup, *The Endangered Species Act: Making Innocent Species the Enemy*. Bozeman, MT: Political Economy Research Center, April 1995.

Ike C. Sugg, "If a Grizzly Attacks, Drop Your Gun," *Wall Street Journal*, June 23, 1993.

John Waithaka, "The Elephant Menace," *Wildlife Conservation*, March/April 1993.

T.H. Watkins, "What's Wrong with the Endangered Species Act? Not Much and Here's Why," *Audubon*, January 1996.

Suzanne Winckler, "Stopgap Measure," *Atlantic Monthly*, January 1992.

Internet Sites

John Burnett, "Guatemala Struggles to Protect Rain Forest from Invaders," May 1998. www.planeta.com.

Virginia Campbell, "Elephants in the Balance: Conserving Africa's Elephants," World Wide Fund for Nature. www.panda.org.

M. Lynne Corn et al., "Harmful Non-Native Species: Issues for Congress," Congressional Research Report for Congress RL30123, April 8, 1999. www.cnie.org.

Defenders of Wildlife, "The Case for Saving Species," *Defenders*, Summer 1995. www.defenders. org.

Brock Evans, "The Endangered Species Coalition: From the Director." www.stopextinction.org.

Whit Gibbons, "No Matter How Endangered, Every Species Should Be Protected," *Online Athens*, November 19, 2000. www.onlineathens.com.

IUCN, "The 2000 IUCN Red List of Threatened Species." www.redlist.org.

Peter Jackson, "A Future for Tigers," *People and the Planet*, no. 4, 1998. www.peopleandplanet.net.

Maquipucuna Foundation, "Academic Resources for Computing and Higher Education Services, University of Georgia," 2001. www.arches.uga.edu.

Massachusetts Sierran Online, April/May 1999. www.sierraclub mass.org.

National Cattlemen's Beef Association, "Lott: ESA Needs Common-Sense Revisions," June 12, 2001. http://hill.beef.org.

Nature Conservancy, "Rio Bravo, Belize." www.nature.org.

North Atlantic Salmon Fund, "North Atlantic Salmon Fund: Working for the Global Restoration of the Wild Atlantic Salmon." www.gamefishing.co.uk.

Jeff Opperman, "The Impacts of Subsidies on Endangered Species," April 1996. www.ti.org.

Randal O'Toole, "The Endangered Endangered Species Act," *Different Drummer,* Winter 1996. www.ti.org.

Programme for Belize, "Explore Rio Bravo," 2001. www.pfbe lize.org.

S. Stuart, "Species: Unprecedented Extinction Rate, and It's Increasing," 2000. www.iucn.org.

J. Sundberg, *NGO Landscapes: Conservation in the Maya Biosphere, Peten Guatemala.* www.planeta.com.

U.S. Fish and Wildlife Service, Delisted Species Reports. http://ecos.fws.gov.

U. S. Fish and Wildlife Service, "Threatened and Endangered Species System (TESS)." http://ecos.fws.gov.

David S. Wilcove et al., "Rebuilding the Ark: Toward a More Effective Endangered Species Act for Private Land," December 5, 1996. www.edf.org.

WildNet Africa, "The Case Against Commercial Trade in Elephant Products," 2001. http://wildnetafrica.co.za.

Others

Nigel Asquith, "Encouraging Private Sector Investment in Biodiversity Conservation Case Studies and a Way Forward," Working Paper. Washington, DC: Conservation International, n. d.

David Cameron, testimony at hearing of the House Committee on Resources, 104th Cong., 1st sess., May 25, 1995.

C.R. Carroll, "Precautionary Approaches: Science and the Balance Between Markets and Regulation," paper presented at the Political Economy Forum, "A Critique of Free Market Environmentalism," Lone Mountain Ranch, Big Sky, Montana, April 2, 2001, sponsored by PERC—The Center for Free Market Environmentalism, Bozeman, MT.

M. Lynne Corn et al., "Endangered Species: Continuing Controversy," Congressional Research Service Issue Brief IB95003, 1995.

Don Coursey, "The Revealed Demand for a Public Good: Evidence from Endangered and Threatened Species," lecture prepared for the American Association for the Advancement of Science annual meeting, January 1994.

C.H. Flather, L.A. Joyce, and C.A. Bloomgarden, "Species Endangerment Patterns in the United States," Washington, DC: USDA, Forest Service. General Technical Report RM-241, January 1994.

R.B. Martin, "Communal Area Management for Indigenous Resources," CAMPFIRE Working Document No. 1/86. Harare, Zimbabwe: Department of National Parks and Wildlife Management, 1986.

Margaret Rector, testimony at hearing of the House Committee on Resources, 104th Cong., 1st sess., March 20, 1996.

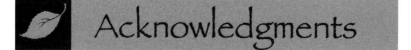

Acknowledgments

Critical Thinking About Environmental Issues: *Endangered Species* by Randy T. Simmons is part of a series designed to take an objective look at emotional environmental issues, such as the danger of losing animals and plants to extinction. The editor of the series, Jane S. Shaw, particularly appreciates the support of two people who recognized the value of treating these issues in a fair, balanced, and thorough way. They are Fred L. Smith Jr., president of the Competitive Enterprise Institute in Washington, D.C., and Terry L. Anderson, executive director of PERC—the Center for Free Market Environmentalism—in Bozeman, MT. She also thanks Michael Sanera for his role in initiating this series.

 Index

Picture Credits

Cover photo: U.S. Fish and Wildlife Service
© Academy of Natural Sciences of Philadelphia/CORBIS, 13, 24
© AFP/CORBIS, 31
© Annie Griffiths Belt/CORBIS, 74
© Bettmann/CORBIS, 17, 50
© Richard Bickel/CORBIS, 83
© Jonathan Blair/CORBIS, 68
© W. Perry Conway/CORBIS, 10
© Corel Corporation, 38, 59, 81
© Digital Stock, 16, 33, 53
© Kevin Fleming/CORBIS, 84
© Michael and Patricia Fogden/CORBIS, 43
© Lowell Georgia/CORBIS, 47
© Dan Guravich/CORBIS, 70
© David G. Houser/CORBIS, 69
© Wolfgang Kaehler/CORBIS, 20
© Larry Lee Photography/CORBIS, 76
© Craig Lovell/CORBIS, 54
© Buddy Mays/CORBIS, 14
© PhotoDisc, 79
© Picture Press/CORBIS, 57
© Programme for Belize, 64, 77
© Reuters NewMedia Inc./CORBIS, 48
© Kevin Schafer/CORBIS, 18
© Paul A. Souders/CORBIS, 23
© Tim Thompson/CORBIS, 36
© Jeff Vanuga/CORBIS, 39
© Kennan Ward/CORBIS, 29, 61
© Ron Watts/CORBIS, 60

About the Author

Randy T. Simmons is Professor and Head of the Political Science Department at Utah State University. He is coauthor with William C. Mitchell of *Beyond Politics: Markets, Welfare, and the Failure of Bureaucracy* (Westview) and coeditor of *Wilderness and Political Ecology* (University of Utah Press). He lives in Providence, Utah, with his wife, Janet Simmons.